The Complete Basketball Coaches' Guide to Footwork, Balance, and Pivoting

John Kimble

ISBN: 978-1-60679-200-1
Library of Congress Control Number: 2011945043
Cover design: Studio J Art & Design
Book layout: Studio J Art & Design
Front cover photo: Howard Smith—US Presswire

Coaches Choice
P.O. Box 1828
Monterey, CA 93942
www.coacheschoice.com

Dedication

It is very easy to become busy with our everyday life and not appreciate the people that matter the most to our personal lives. I would like to take this opportunity to dedicate this particular book to my wife, Pat, for the commitment she has made in raising our children, as well as being a loving and supportive spouse. Being a wife and a parent of two children is tough enough in today's times, but being a teacher as well as a coach's wife and a fantastic mother is many times more difficult. Taking over some of my parental responsibilities while I was absent because of coaching did not go unnoticed nor unappreciated by me or by our children. Being such a great example and making all the sacrifices she made to provide both children with great childhoods and successful adult lives is appreciated by all three of us. Without her many commitments and sacrifices, their core values and characters and their careers might not exist. Mom, wife, and supporter—thank you from our entire family.

Acknowledgments

This book is dedicated to all of those who have influenced my basketball coaching life and to all the committed basketball coaches who have spent countless hours at coaching clinics, reading books, and "X-ing and O-ing" it with their colleagues. I have been a player, a fan, a teacher of the game, a student of the game, a coach, and a lover of the game. As a student and a coach of the game, several influences have impacted my coaching beliefs. These influences range from summer basketball camps, coaching clinics, coaching textbooks and written publications, videotapes, observing other coaches' practices, and the countless informal coaching clinics with many other coaches trying to learn just one more drill, defense, or play.

Personal influences in my coaching life have come from many of the most top-notch coaches of the game: The Iowa Basketball Camp (Lute Olson and Scott Thompson), The Doug Collins Basketball Camp (Doug Collins and Bob Sullivan), The University of Illinois Basketball Camp (Dick Nagy and Lou Henson), The Indiana Basketball Camp (Bob Knight), The Dick Baumgartner Shooting Camp (Dick Baumgartner), The Washington State University Cougar Cage Camp (George Raveling, Tom Pugliese, Mark Edwards, and Jim Livengood), The Snow Valley Basketball School (Herb Livesey), The Notre Dame University Basketball Camp (Digger Phelps and Danny Nee), The Illinois State University Basketball Camp (Tom Richardson), The Millikin University Basketball Camp (Joe Ramsey), Eastern Illinois University (Don Eddy), The Purdue University Basketball Camp (Lee Rose), The Oregon State University Basketball Camp (Ralph Miller and Lanny Van Eman), The Troy State University Basketball Camp (Don Maestri), The Maryville (TN) College Basketball Camp (Randy Lambert), and The Kansas State University Basketball Camp (Jim Wooldridge, Mike Miller, Jimmy Elgas, Charles Baker, and Chad Altadonna). Just a few of the most memorable and outstanding speakers I have heard at some of the many coaching clinics I have attended include: Coach Lute Olson, Coach Doug Collins, Coach Hubie Brown, Coach Bob Knight, Coach Dick Nagy, Coach Don Meyers, and Coach Rick Majerus.

The most outstanding authors of coaching books include: Coach Del Harris, Coach Dean Smith, Coach Bob Knight, and Coach Fran Webster. Coach Lute Olson, Coach Hubie Brown, Coach Don Meyer and Coach Jerry Krause, Coach Del Harris, and Coach Dick Baumgartner have been authors of some of the most outstanding videotapes I have observed and from which I have learned a great deal. Coaching colleagues with whom I have worked include: Doug Collins, Brian James, Gerry Thornton, Benny Gabbard, Steve Gould, Bob Sullivan, Norm Frazier, Tom Wierzba, Steve Laur, Ron

Roher, Will Rey, Mike Davis, Dennis Kagel, Don Eiker, Bob Trimble, Dave Toler, and Ed Butkovich. I was fortunate to always be involved with tremendous coaching staffs with outstanding coaches, who were even more outstanding as people and friends to me than as coaches. These good friends include such outstanding people as: Benny Gabbard, Mitch Buckelew, Scott Huerkamp, Phil Barbara, Chris Martello, Don Tanney, Les Wilson, Al Cornish, Ron Lowery, John Lenz, Doug Zehr, and Ken Maye. To all of these people, I say, "Thank you for your loyalty, commitment, hard work, and effort!"

I would like to say thanks to the many players I have coached, to the extraordinary non-player students who were big parts of the basketball programs—the managers, the student statisticians, the film-takers, the student athletic trainers, and student helpers. I hope that I conveyed to each and every one of them the fact that they were important parts of the program and that they all deserved credit for the successes of the basketball programs of which they were a part.

I want to also say thank you to the adults whom I have met and become friends with in the different communities where I have coached. These are people who participated in the development and the successes of the basketball programs where I coached. These people were contributors, supporters of the program, faithful fans, and loyal friends. Some were parents of players, while some were parents of students, and some were just fans of the game. These people include: Bob and Ro Flannagan, Ed and Roseanne Moore, Ron and Mary Roher, Dick and Sharon Payne, Don and Bev Hiter, Dave Gregory, Norm Frazier, John and Pam Russell, Ken and Judy Sunderland, Fred Prager, Mark Henry, Carlan and Dee Dee Martin, George Stakely, Charles Owens, Dutch VanBuskirk, Kelly Stanford, Junior Robertson, Bobby Johnson, June Carter, Greg Cadenhead, Greg and Darla Southard, and so many other good people.

This book is also dedicated to those who have influenced my personal life. I was raised by inspirational parents who always taught me to go the extra step, to never be satisfied until the job was done right. I hope I have succeeded in accomplishing that goal with the writing of this book. My wife, Pat, was my biggest source of encouragement to write this book. She was my constant positive reinforcement and support. My daughter Emily and son Adam also, who helped me continue this endeavor, were sources of personal encouragement. My two brothers, Joe and Jim, also offered support as I slowly progressed through the ordeal of organizing and writing. My parents were always positive role models and constant sources of encouragement and support. Gerry Thornton, longtime friend and fellow student of the game, has affected my coaching career probably more than any other person; while Benny Gabbard was the one person who got me started in my junior college coaching career and showed great faith and confidence in me in my first years of coaching junior college basketball. While coaching together at the junior college level, Coach Gabbard was the one coach who influenced me to adopt the speed game style of play. Coach Don Meyer has been a helpful, encouraging, and supportive friend as well as a tremendous example in being a great coach and a great person. Jerry Krause (friend, coach at Gonzaga University, author, and an invaluable source of information) also was of great help and encouragement, as was Kevin Newell (senior editor of *Scholastic Coach* and *Athletic Director*, supporter, and friend), Murray Pool (former high school coach and current publisher of *Basketball Sense*, friend, and source of information), and Mike Podoll (editor of *Winning Hoops* basketball magazine).

Foreword

It is my pleasure to offer some comments on John Kimble's book on footwork. As always, Coach Kimble's latest book is again detailed, organized, and laid out so that it can be effectively used by every coach who reads his book. Every detail of every phase of the game is thoroughly covered and discussed.

I always listen carefully to Coach Knight when he offers advice on teaching the game of basketball. Coach Bob Knight has often said that footwork is the most undertaught phase of the game of basketball.

This book allows you the opportunity to learn about footwork from A to Z. You will find teaching points and coaching phrases that will fit your philosophy of teaching and coaching the game. One size does not fit all, and this book does not try to adamantly sell any one system of footwork.

As Morgan Wootten often says, "We get what we emphasize and not what we teach." These new insights and techniques into the teaching of footwork will help your team be more explosive, cut down on turnovers, and have confidence on both ends of the floor.

Good luck with your team and the teaching of footwork.

Don Meyer
Former Head Men's Basketball Coach
Northern State University

Contents

Introduction

As players become more and more proficient in strength, quickness, speed, and overall athletic ability, it is the job of coaches at every level of play to make sure that their players do not become deficient in the overall basketball fundamentals that are a prerequisite for the ultimate success of their team. As the game seems to desire flashy play and exciting plays to highlight and accentuate the athletic talents of today's players, it is still the basic fundamentals of the game (that seem to be unnecessary and boring for some players to learn and for some coaches to teach and emphasize) that are sometimes the missing pieces for the ultimate overall success of the team.

The elementary skill of pivoting is one of those fundamentals whose importance seems to be taken much too lightly. Pivoting is an important and necessary component of basketball skills that coaches and players alike often call one of the fundamentals of the game. The art of pivoting is an integral part of many facets of offensive basketball. These include passing the basketball and shooting the basketball off the dribble as well as off the pass. Pivoting should be an important part of offensive post play. Pivoting is a vital part of the numerous types of action that take place after the various types of screens are set. Just one of the many ways that pivoting is also a valuable component of defensive basketball is that it is a part of defensive boxing out as well as the actual rebounding of the basketball.

The skill of pivoting is the initial part of a player getting in triple-threat position after catching a pass (to become a shooter, dribbler, or passer). Pivoting is essential in successfully executing aggressive moves as an offensive post player. Pivoting is a major component of setting any type of screens for offensive teammates. The skill of pivoting is a requirement to be able to successfully rebound the basketball both offensively as well as defensively. To become an on-the-ball aggressive defensive player, pivoting is essential. To stop a dribbler from attacking the front foot, a player must be able to reverse pivot.

Each of the six phases of the game—ball handling, shooting, offensive post play, rebounding, screening, and defending—have a full chapter devoted to the details of pivoting that make that particular fundamental become a solid technique in a player's overall basketball repertoire (Chapters 2 through 7). The specific pivoting details to learn, practice, and improve those fundamentals are addressed in those chapters, which include nearly 200 diagrams of the action, specific footwork, and format of many drills that can be used to learn and practice the various techniques of the different phases of the game.

Chapter 1 gives an overall philosophy on how to effectively teach players offenses and defenses. An in-depth philosophy on how to incorporate drills into the practice setting that will be productive as well as time-efficient is stressed. This chapter also organizes a portion of the daily practice so that the fundamental skills described in this book, as well as other skills, can be incorporated into the format of each practice, while being as time efficient as it can possibly be.

Throughout, the book reiterates why the art of pivoting is so important to the successful execution of any individual or team fundamental. Reasons are given why pivoting is so vital to the wins you hope to achieve.

Also included with this book is a companion DVD that should serve not as a substitute but as a supplement to the book. Together, it is hoped that both of these media help illustrate the overall importance of footwork in the game of basketball and help coaches teach the relevant skills and techniques better.

Have a great season.

Diagram Examples

The following sample diagrams illustrate elements that will be used throughout the diagrams in the book.

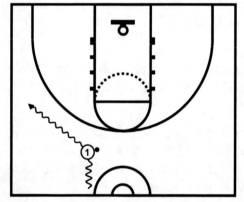

Offensive player 01 dribbling the ball.

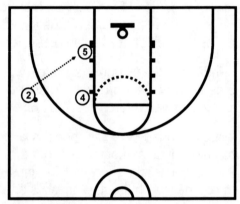

Offensive player 02 passing the ball to post player 05.

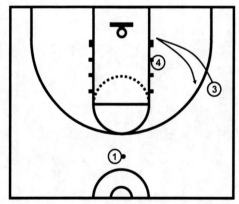

03 cutting to get open to receive the ball from 01.

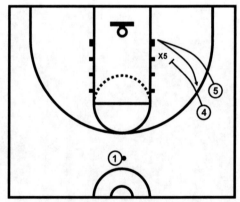

04 screening 05's defender (X5) to get him open to receive the pass from 01.

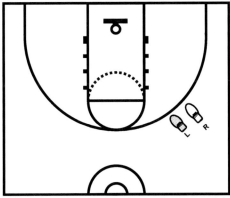

Offensive player with the ball whose right foot is the free foot and (shaded) left foot is the pivot foot.

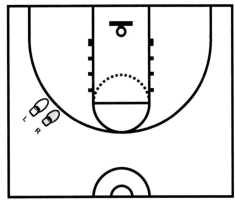

Offensive player with the ball whose left foot is the free foot and (shaded) right foot is the pivot foot.

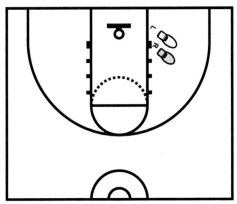

Post player with the ball whose left foot is the free foot and (shaded) right foot is the pivot foot.

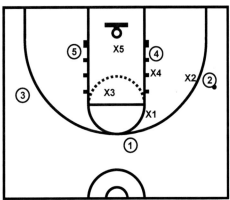

Defenders X1, X2, X3, X4, and X5 guarding their offensive opponents 01, 02, 03, 04, and 05, respectively.

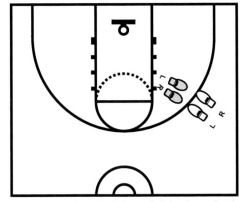

Defensive player's left and right foot (both shaded) and offensive player's left and right foot (not shaded).

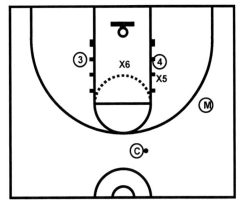

Coach (C) and manager (M) in a breakdown drill with two offensive players (04 and 03) and two defensive players (X5 and X6).

1

Teaching Methods and Philosophy on Drills

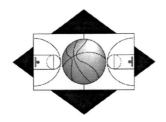

"Failing to prepare is preparing to fail."
—Coach John Wooden

Teaching Fundamentals, Techniques, and Offenses by Utilizing Drills

Countless fundamentals, skills, techniques, and concepts must be taught to each individual basketball player as well as to the overall team. Many fundamentals and techniques strictly apply to the offensive phase of the game. The defensive portion of the game includes numerous individual and team concepts, skills and techniques, and fundamental footwork that must be taught to each player and the team.

A team is only as strong as its weakest link. An individual player is only as strong as his mastery of the basic fundamentals of the basketball skills necessary for success. Therefore, countless techniques must be taught to each player in order to maximize each player's skill level. When each player's skill levels are maximized, it makes the team a stronger and more cohesive unit. Unfortunately, practice time is a significant constraint to the amount of teaching by coaching staffs and the amount of learning by the players.

A seemingly unlimited amount of material must be taught to players in a limited period of time. This task can be difficult for a coaching staff to perform.

For a coach to be successful, he must be an excellent teacher. He must have a fundamentally sound concept of how to convey what needs to be taught to his players and to motivate those players to learn the fundamentals.

The coach must teach the proper techniques to the players. He must show the players how those techniques are to be performed. Players also expect to know why they are to perform tasks, not just that they are to do them.

If coaches want the players to successfully execute those skills and techniques, coaches must confirm to players the importance of proper techniques, demonstrate to players how to perform those skills, and provide game-realistic settings for players to practice, improve, and perfect those skills and techniques.

One particular coaching philosophy is a belief that in order for a basketball program to be successful, coaches must demand that every player be fundamentally sound in how to perform all techniques of the game. The coaching staff must be able to motivate every player in performing those fundamentals at their highest level of intensity.

Attention to detail by the coaching staff is crucial, as well as the positive and constructive criticism that must come with the teaching and the drill work. Game-realistic scenarios must be implemented to simulate game-like conditions. Drills must be created to practice the various offensive and defensive skills and techniques.

The old cliché, "Practice makes perfect," should not apply in your program. The philosophy should be: "*Perfect* practice makes perfect!"

Success will come in small, consistent increments so that players' confidence in themselves, in their teammates, and in the system will slowly grow and increase as time goes on The whole-part-whole teaching method (with a great emphasis on the how and the why on every technique, every skill, whether it is offense, defense, or transition) gives the best results. Players must have confidence that the methods and techniques they are being taught are the best possible ways for them to be successful. The manner in which the skills are being taught to the players should give the players assurance they will be able to successfully perform those skills.

In basketball, games can be won in many ways. Coaches can utilize many different teaching methods and support numerous styles of play. For the team to have confidence and trust in the coaching staff, the coaching staff must be students of the game. After carefully choosing the specific techniques, methods, and styles of how to play the game, the coaching staff must convey that strong belief and confidence to each and every team member. Then and only then will players be sold on the philosophy of the staff. The players will give their heart and soul to the program and play with the needed intensity in order to be successful. Players must believe in what they are doing (whether it is a type of technique, an offense, a defense, a play, or whatever they are performing), if they are to perform at a high degree of intensity. With that high level of intensity often comes the success of the players.

When something new, such as a new offense, is introduced to the team, the offense should be introduced as a whole entity. Then, the offense can be broken down to the basics that are needed for the offense to be successful. The specific techniques required for the offense to be able to operate efficiently and successfully should then be demonstrated. Those particular skills in game-realistic drills are worked on only after the players have graduated to that particular level of performance.

The first drills that are taught and practiced are more teaching drills than intense and competitive drills. The first drills are actually broken down and have levels of skill and learning competencies that all players must accomplish before they get to the high-level skill performance drills.

Whole-Part-Whole Teaching Method

In the phrase whole-part-whole method of teaching, the whole is the entire play (or concept) that is being introduced. All five players participate in this phase. The parts are the specific techniques performed by each of the five players. Each player has different skills and techniques that must be performed in order for the play to be successful. A part could be just one player working on learning, understanding, and executing one simple task that takes place in just one specific situation. The part could be one player performing several tasks in a wider range scenario, or the part could be five players doing several tasks simultaneously.

For instance, if you are introducing a new continuity offense to the team, the coaching staff should first show the team the entire offensive continuity. The staff would have five players demonstrate the offense by walking them through the offense, while the remaining players observe. Then, the staff would rotate other players into the offense until all have gone through the offense. Coaches would have two groups of players go through the offense at higher degrees of speed, until game speed is reached. No defense is used, and no shots would be taken, so that the continuity offense could be run for longer periods of time, without any interruptions.

Coaches should not allow any distractions during this learning phase. Once the basic movement patterns and rules are learned by all team members, coaches would work on all players practicing their shots from the spots they would get their shots during the game.

Coaches would demonstrate where and how the shooters would receive passes to get their shots. Coaches would have the players practice those shots and have other players practice the passes they would make to those shooters (from the same locations on the court that they would in a game). Coaches should remember that every drill must be as game-realistic as possible.

Once the players learn their specific passing and shot locations and they start feeling comfortable with understanding the offense, the level of intensity of the breakdown drills is stepped up. Goals and performance standards are established, with these goals and standards increasing in difficulty as the players progress in their skill development and knowledge of the concept being introduced.

As a coach, it is best not to assume every player has mastered all of the fundamental skills of basketball. The more elementary the coach is in the initial breakdown drills before advancing to more sophisticated breakdown drills, the more solid his players will be in their overall understanding, performance level, and success of whatever skill is being taught and performed.

The more experience the players obtain, the more demanding the coaching staff can be with them. No drill should be too easy or too difficult. Coaching staffs should remember to start at the very basic fundamentals and lay a strong foundation before amping up the degree of difficulty (and, therefore, the amount of game realism). The whole should gradually and ultimately be the performance of all five players in a game, but that will take time, planning, teaching, practicing, drilling, effort, and patience on the part of both the coaches and the players.

Following are some points of emphasis a coaching staff should keep in mind while using the whole-part-whole teaching method in their basketball practices:

- Remember that the gymnasium is the classroom. In order for learning to take place in any classroom, the staff must provide organization and an atmosphere conducive for learning. Have discipline in the classroom. Demand that players pay attention and concentrate when teaching is going on. Encourage questions from players at the appropriate times.
- Don't assume that players possess the fundamental skills that are necessary for them to be successful. It is better to overteach the fundamentals than to make assumptions and overrate the players' talent and skill levels.
- Don't assume the players possess knowledge they may not have. Making assumptions of players' ability level and knowledge of the game can be disastrous for all parties involved.
- Have an organized practice plan; it is a coach's lesson plan. Plan your work, and work your plan. Don't vary too much from your plan, but have some flexibility in it, also. Don't be bound by the plan. Learn what a teaching moment is, and take advantage of those opportunities, even if it means varying from the practice plan.
- Make sure the time limits of all drills are short enough that players do not get bored with the same drill. A coach should run a drill for four or five minutes three different times in a practice versus a 15-minute drill at one setting.
- Make sure that players are not standing at the end of lines during drills, where the attention and intensity levels can wane. Create your drills where everyone is involved, not just three or four players at a time.

- Make sure all breakdown drills have gradual levels of difficulty. As players improve, both physically and mentally, they need to graduate to a more difficult level. This approach allows the positive reinforcement players need as they initially learn and develop skills and techniques. It also keeps the focus of players later on as they improve their skills.
- Set realistic performance goals for your players in the various practice drills. Make the goals a realistic similarity to the tough competition of games.
- Keep statistics on the performances of players in practice. Reward the winners in small ways, and give small penalties for the losing individuals or groups.
- Demand from your players and assistant coaches a quick transition from one drill to the next. Don't let anyone waste time in the rotation from one drill to another. This approach creates a mindset for more productive and time efficient practices.
- Involve your assistant coaches in the practice planning and the actual teaching on the court. Get them involved in the practice planning sessions, and listen to their ideas. Let them coach *when* they are prepared.
- Make sure that the more sophisticated drills that are utilized are game-realistic. The higher level drills always must be performed at game speed and have some forms of pressure and competition placed on the players. These drills will result in winners and losers with awards and (minimal) penalties.
- If a coach wants his players to be enthusiastic and energetic, he must not only be enthusiastic and energetic, but must be the most enthusiastic and energetic person in the gym. The head coach must be an example to the coaching staff and to all players. If you are the head coach, you must be the leader and set an example for all to follow. Let the players and assistant coaches feed off your energy and enthusiasm.
- Don't accept anything but excellence from yourself, your staff, or your players. Players and assistant coaches will improve only if they are self-motivated or are pushed by others.
- Have a keen eye for detail. Look for the most minute techniques and methods, and expect proper execution from your players on every technique that is being taught. Include points of emphasis and coaching points in your practice plan, with your assistant coaches and with your players in practice.
- Be positive when correcting players. Be critical in a positive way. Be demanding when it comes to your players' attention and physical effort. Don't accept anything below that high level of concentration and mental effort. Especially praise the team and the strong efforts of individual players who make those strong and positive efforts. Let the players know that you are well aware of the hustle and effort of every player on the court.
- Teach the rules of the game to your players. Teams cannot succeed unless the rules of the game are followed, and rules cannot be followed unless the rules are taught by coaches and learned by players.

Expectations

Ultimately, remember that a great coach must be a great teacher. A great teacher must be a great student. He must know the material he is teaching. He must stay up with the game. Coaches must stay informed of the changes of styles, techniques, and rules of the game. Basketball is not a static game. Changes occur constantly during every game. Coaches must have high levels of expectations from the assistant coaches, the players, the managers, and above all, from himself. Oftentimes, people only reach minimum levels that they expect of themselves. Coaches should have high expectations of every player, but coaches cannot expect anyone in the program to perform at a higher level than he performs. Coaches are models to everyone in the program every minute of every day—be a strong example and model.

Every athletic team has practice to prepare for their games. What occurs in practice will make the difference whether the team will succeed or fail in the game.

A significant portion of each of the daily practices should be the fundamental drills that will be discussed. Drills and the manner in which they are taught and how they are incorporated into the daily practices will determine whether a coach is successful and whether the team has an opportunity to succeed in actual competition. The techniques and methods that a coaching staff chooses to teach are very important to the success of that team. The effort to make sure that all fundamentals are taught, developed, and practiced is of tremendous importance to the overall success of that team.

Specific Techniques of the Game

Various types of passes are necessary for the many different man and zone offenses to be successful. Passes are taught and demonstrated and then practiced in repetitive forms under game-like conditions. The different types of dribbling are constantly practiced in various drills that are constructed with as much game realism as possible. The different types of man and zone offense cuts are also explained, demonstrated, and practiced on when and how the cuts can be most effective within the offense.

Drills should be utilized to work on the proper screening techniques utilized in both man and zone offenses. Post-up moves should be practiced individually (for both post as well as perimeter players)—with and without defensive opposition daily.

Individual drills and team drills help players become more proficient in the overall skill of offensive rebounding. Techniques of overcoming defensive box-outs, reading the flight of the ball on missed shots, and anticipating where the offensive rebounds will fall must be practiced for players to become proficient in the art of offensive rebounding.

Countless types of shooting drills should be introduced and used several times in each daily practice so that shooters can become more proficient shooters both on the interior and on the perimeter of the offenses that each team possesses in its offensive arsenal. Techniques of catching the basketball (while in shooting position so that shooters can get their shots off more quickly) are also a daily part of the shooting practice routines.

Six Individual Offensive Skills

Coaches should have the following six main categories of individual player offensive skill breakdown drills in their offensive drill package:
- Basic fundamentals station drills
- Shooting drills
- Dribbling drills
- Pivoting, passing, and catching drills
- Offensive rebounding drills
- Transition drills

The following is a philosophical composite of all of the drills that have emerged from many years of coaching basketball, baseball, and football at the high school level, and also coaching basketball at the junior college level. The philosophy has also developed from observing practices from some of the top coaches at the high school, college, and NBA levels. Ideas were taken and sometimes modified (from these coaches at their practices, at summer camps, coaching clinics, books, and videotapes) to fit that team's level of play and competition.

Philosophy on Drills

Successful basketball coaches must not only be great teachers and motivators, but also must have tools and instruments that will allow their players to learn the skills and techniques, and also allow them to improve on the actual skill levels. Player's skills can be improved by a watchful and detail-mined coaching staff. Successful basketball coaches must always remember the following:
- Make practices as game-realistic as possible. Have fundamental drills and breakdown drills incorporated in all phases of the game. Teach at your practices.
- Have an environment that is conducive to learning (for the players) and teaching (for the coaching staff). Remember that the practice facility is the basketball coach's classroom.
- Pay attention to all details in every drill and with every player.
- Get excited as a coach. Be enthusiastic. You must love to come to practice for the players to love to come. Players must be able to see you love to teach the game. Be thorough in your teaching. Assume that your players know nothing. Be a stickler for the smallest of details (in a positive manner). Do not ask for, but demand full efforts from yourself, your coaching staff, and your players.

- Be a great teacher and motivator.
- Have a detailed practice plan and follow it. Plan your work, and work your plan. Still, at times you must be flexible with your practice plan when special occurrences demand it.
- Incorporate the whole-part-whole method in your teaching of the game.
- Do not ask for, but demand your players' attention. Players must give coaches their eyes and ears at all times.
- Make practices more demanding and tougher (both physically and mentally) than the games will demand.
- Establish drills so that the players must concentrate as they perform them. This approach will prepare them so that they will be able to focus more effectively in their games.
- Do not allow any players to stand around in practice, doing nothing. Keep all players and coaches involved during all drills.
- Assume that players know nothing and that they have no fundamental skills. Start with the basics both intellectually and skill-wise. Stress fundamentals and proper technique. Stress mental and physical effort all of the time by every player.
- Emphasize teamwork both on offense and defense. Stress communication between teammates and coaching staffs.
- Give positive credit to players with enthusiasm, especially when they have shown extra effort, physically or mentally.
- Send a player for a water break when he does something positive a number of times. Have the other players shoot one-and-one free throws. If a player misses the front end of the one-and-one, have him run a full-court sprint. If a player makes the front end of the one-and-one, but misses the second free throw, have that player run a half-court sprint. If a player makes both ends of a one-and-one, send him for water, also. Be consistent with rewards and punishments.
- Consistently reward the player or players who perform correctly, rather than always punishing the player or players who do not perform as successfully.
- Allow for ample running and movement activities immediately before you send your players to shoot free throws. Make sure you have your players shoot two free throws at a time, as the players would do in a game.
- Make each drill a great drill. A drill is not a good drill, unless the coach teaches the drill in a great manner.
- Constructively correct a player when he commits an error, and try not to criticize that player. Be sure that all criticisms are constructive and not personal, and make certain the player understands this.
- Set standards for your players in your shooting drills. Set time limits for your players to hurry (but to always be under control) and get off as many shots as possible. Set accuracy limits for your players as well. A specific number of shots must be taken and a specific number of shots must be made during each different shooting drill.

- Utilize many of your shooting drills (particularly free throw shooting drills) after some type of strenuous drill. Your players will get accustomed to shooting when they are winded and fatigued.
- Make sure you can combine drills so that frequent opportunities are available to work on offense-to-defense transition, as well as defense-to-offense transition.
- Have managers record players' statistics from your practice. Post those statistics, so that players can see their results are important to you and the team. Have standards set for individuals as well as for the team. Have winners and losers with the respective awards and penalties.
- Organize your drills to include a variety of competition: individual competition, small group competition, and team competition. Have a winner and a loser in the majority of the competitive drills, with the losers having some form of light penalty. The light penalty could be in the form of small sprints, push-ups, or sit-ups.
- Critique each player in a fair but positive manner. When a coach is about to criticize a player, first ask him, "What did you just do correctly?" Then ask him, "What did you do incorrectly?"
- Do not allow yourself to omit the physical conditioning of your players. Make some of your drills also involve conditioning.
- Use a practice plan as a guideline to manage the practice time, realizing on-the-court adjustments and variations may need to be made to the practice plan. "Practice does not make perfect," but "*Perfect* practice does make perfect." Perfect practice comes from well-planned practice plans by the coaching staff. The practice plan is the coach's lesson plan.
- Implement a great deal of structure into your practice plans and practice routines so your players can anticipate what to expect. Keep the practice lengths consistent, with shorter practices and lighter physical activity the night before games and often the night after games.
- On a rare occasion, call off a scheduled practice. During the long, hard, grueling part of the season about halfway or two thirds or so through the schedule, this mental and physical break can sometimes get life back into the players' legs and intensity level. Or, a coaching staff can still have practice, but have practice planned in a completely different manner. Play volleyball or Wiffle® ball in the gym or watch a movie or have pizza for the team with the coaching staff. It can be a positive diversion and a good mental break for the players, as well as the coaches.
- Teach the following phrase by preaching it as well as by demonstrating by example: "Failing to prepare is preparing to fail."
- Do not end any drill on a negative note. Do not conclude a scrimmage on a missed shot or a turnover. Never finish a shooting drill on a missed shot.
- Do not finish your practice with conditioning work. Conditioning is extremely important, but it need not conclude a practice. The last drill or activity should be a positive and rewarding type of activity for the players to give them the motivation for the next day's practice. Make them eager for tomorrow's practice.

These thoughts and ideas have been taken from other coaches or have been discovered over the years. Coaches can integrate them into their own philosophy and practice sessions with the expectation of remarkable results.

DRILLS

Offensive fundamentals such as passing, catching, screening, cutting, dribbling, rebounding, and shooting must be practiced with a great deal of effort, concentration, detail, intensity, and numerous repetitions. This section includes a daily pre-practice routine for basic fundamentals and stretching, followed by various types of shooting drills that can be used to not only work on shooting fundamentals, but maintain the high level of intensity and focus that is a requirement of all players.

Also described are offensive pivoting and passing breakdown drills and offensive rebounding drills, as well as two transition drills that are extremely important for all half-court offenses to be successful. Even though man and zone offenses are primarily thought of in a half-court offense mindset, transition from defense to a specific offense and, conversely, transition from offense back to defense should be greatly emphasized. Transition should be an integral part of the foundation of any offense and defense.

Daily Pre-Practice Routine for Basic Fundamentals and Stretching

This pre-practice fundamental and stretching routine (Table 1-1) is designed for two 12-man teams to be able to operate at the same time on the same court (that has two main goals and two side baskets on opposite sides of the main court. Twenty-four players can be involved at the same time in this routine in a gymnasium that has two main basketball goals and four supplemental side court goals. Each player needs to have his own basketball. Two energetic and mobile coaches serve as observers, correcting, motivating, encouraging, coaching, and above all, teaching of all players involved.

Each player works on stretching so they will be prepared for upcoming practices as well as the many different fundamental skills that are necessary for individual players and teams to be successful. This routine allows for short but concentrated time periods to work on a wide range of fundamentals. The techniques worked on are a requirement if you are to build fundamentally sound basketball players.

This pre-practice routine also sets the tone for an upbeat practice, while also forcing every player to concentrate on his individual and group responsibilities. This routine has no room for boredom and standing around, as many activities last only 30 seconds up to one minute. Only a couple of drills last more than the typical one minute, and those

Score Clock	Duration (Minutes)	Accumulated Time (Minutes)	Varsity Routine Two-Man and Three-Man Groups for the Varsity Players		Junior Varsity Routine Two-Man and Three-Man Groups for the Junior Varsity Players	
			(1A, 1B) (2A, 2B) (3A, 11) [1A, 2A, 3A] [1B, 2B, 11]	(3B, 4A) (4B, 5A) (5B, 12) [4A, 5A, 5B] [3B, 4B, 12]	(1A, 1B) (2A, 2B) (3A, 11) [1A, 2A, 3A] [1B, 2B, 11]	(3B, 4A) (4B, 5A) (5B, 12) [4A, 5A, 5B] [3B, 4B, 12]
42	1	0	• Ankle stretch • Yogi/butterfly stretch (Areas 1 & 3)	• Ankle stretch • Yogi/butterfly stretch (Areas 2 & 4)	• Hesitation dribble • Front crossover dribble (Dribbling line 8)	• Hesitation dribble • Front crossover dribble (Dribbling line 9)
41	1	1	• Hurdle stretch (left) • Hurdle stretch (right) (Area 1)	• Hurdle stretch (left) • Hurdle stretch (right) (Area 2)	• Through legs • Behind back (Dribbling line 8)	• Through legs • Behind back (Dribbling line 9)
40	1	2	• Quad stretch • Finger tips (Area 1)	• Quad stretch • Finger tips (Area 2)	Show-and-go-opposite power moves (Left and right hands) (Baskets 1-2-3)	Show-and-go-opposite power moves (Left and right hands) (Baskets 4-5-6)
39	1	3	• Back stretch • Lie-on-back technique: shooting (Area 1)	• Back stretch • Lie-on-back technique: shooting (Area 2)	Up-and-under power moves (Left and right hands) (Baskets 1-2-3)	Up-and-under power moves (Left and right hands) (Baskets 4-5-6)
38	1	4	• V-cuts • High-leg easy jog (Areas 1 & 3)	• V-cuts • High-leg easy jog (Areas 2 & 4)	Whirl power moves (Left and right hands) (Baskets 1-2-3)	Whirl power moves (Left and right hands) (Baskets 4-5-6)
37	1	5	Basket education (Left and right hand) (Baskets 1-2-3)	Basket education (Left and right hand) (Baskets 4-5-6)	Offensive rebounding technique drill (Areas 3 & 4)	Offensive rebounding technique drill (Areas 5 & 6)
36	1	6	Rebound snatch (off of wall nearest their goal)	Mikan shooting drill (Left/right hand) (Baskets 1-6)	Pride drill (Areas 3 & 4)	Pride drill (Areas 5 & 6)
35	1	7	Mikan shooting drill (Left/right hand) (Baskets 1 thru 6)	Rebound snatch (off of wall nearest their goal)	Pride drill (Areas 3 & 4)	Pride drill (Areas 5 & 6)

Table 1-1

Score Clock	Duration (Minutes)	Accumulated Time (Minutes)	Varsity Routine Two-Man and Three-Man Groups for the Varsity Players		Junior Varsity Routine Two-Man and Three-Man Groups for the Junior Varsity Players	
			(1A, 1B) (2A, 2B) (3A, 11) [1A, 2A, 3A] [1B, 2B, 11]	(3B, 4A) (4B, 5A) (5B, 12) [4A, 5A, 5B] [3B, 4B, 12]	(1A, 1B) (2A, 2B) (3A, 11) [1A, 2A, 3A] [1B, 2B, 11]	(3B, 4A) (4B, 5A) (5B, 12) [4A, 5A, 5B] [3B, 4B, 12]
34	1	8	Baby hook shots Left/right hand (Baskets 1-6)	Wolf defensive drill (Area 7)	Run-and-jump defensive and offensive drill (Area 3)	Run-and-jump defensive and offensive drill (Area 4)
33	1	9	Wolf defensive drill (Area 7)	Baby hook shots (Left/right hand) (Baskets 1-6)	Run-and-jump defensive and offensive drill (Area 3)	Run-and-jump defensive and offensive drill (Area 4)
32	1	10	Pivot and pass: Passer (Areas 3 & 4)	Pivot and pass: Passer (Areas 5 & 6)	Dot shots (Left/right side with no fake) (Baskets 1-2-3)	Dot shots (Left/right side with no fake) (Baskets 4-5-6)
31	1	11	Pivot and pass: Defender (Areas 3 & 4)	Pivot and pass: Defender (Areas 5 & 6)	Dot shots (Left/right side with one fake) (Baskets 1-2-3)	Dot shots (Left/right side with one fake) (Baskets 4-5-6)
30	1	12	Pivot and pass: Pass receiver (Areas 3 & 4)	Pivot and pass: Pass receiver (Areas 5 & 6)	Dot shots (Left/right side with two fakes) (Baskets 1-2-3)	Dot shots (Left/right side with two fakes) (Baskets 4-5-6)
29	1	13	• Hesitation dribble • Front crossover dribble (Dribbling line 8)	• Hesitation dribble • Front crossover dribble (Dribbling line 9)	• Ankle stretch • Yogi/butterfly stretch (Areas 1 & 3)	• Ankle stretch • Yogi/butterfly stretch (Areas 2 & 4)
28	1	14	• Through legs • Behind back (Dribbling line 8)	• Through legs • Behind back (Dribbling line 9)	• Hurdle stretch (left) • Hurdle stretch (right) (Area 1)	• Hurdle stretch (left) • Hurdle stretch (right) (Area 2)
27	1	15	Show-and-go-opposite power moves (Left and right side) (Baskets 1-2-3)	Show-and-go-opposite power moves (Left and right side) (Baskets 4-5-6)	• Quad stretch • Finger tips (Area 1)	• Quad stretch • Finger tips (Area 2)

Table 1-1 (cont.)

Score Clock	Duration (Minutes)	Accumulated Time (Minutes)	Varsity Routine Two-Man and Three-Man Groups for the Varsity Players		Junior Varsity Routine Two-Man and Three-Man Groups for the Junior Varsity Players	
			(1A, 1B) (2A, 2B) (3A, 11) [1A, 2A, 3A] [1B, 2B, 11]	(3B, 4A) (4B, 5A) (5B, 12) [4A, 5A, 5B] [3B, 4B, 12]	(1A, 1B) (2A, 2B) (3A, 11) [1A, 2A, 3A] [1B, 2B, 11]	(3B, 4A) (4B, 5A) (5B, 12) [4A, 5A, 5B] [3B, 4B, 12]
26	1	16	Up-and-under power moves (Left and right side) (Baskets 1-2-3)	Up-and-under power moves (Left and right side) (Baskets 4-5-6)	• Back stretch • Lie-on-back technique: shooting (Area 1)	• Back stretch • Lie-on-back technique: shooting (Area 2)
25	1	17	Whirl power moves (Left and right side) (Baskets 1-2-3)	Whirl power moves (Left and right side) (Baskets 4-5-6)	• V-cuts • High-leg easy jog (Areas 1 & 3)	• V-cuts • High-leg easy jog (Areas 2 & 4)
24	1	18	Offensive rebounding technique drill (Areas 3 & 4)	Offensive rebounding technique drill (Areas 5 & 6)	Basket education (Left and right hand) (Baskets 1-2-3)	Basket education (Left and right hand) (Baskets 4-5-6)
23	1	19	Pride drill (Areas 3 & 4)	Pride drill (Areas 5 & 6)	Rebound snatch (off of wall nearest their goal)	Mikan drill (Left/right hand) (Baskets 1-6)
22	1	20	Pride drill (Areas 3 & 4)	Pride drill (Areas 5 & 6)	Mikan drill (Left/right hand) (Baskets 1-6)	Rebound snatch (off of wall nearest their goal)
21	1	21	Run-and-jump defensive and offensive drill (Area 3)	Run-and-jump defensive and offensive drill (Area 4)	Baby hook shots (Left/right hand) (Baskets 1-6)	Wolf defensive drill (Area 7)
20	1	22	Run-and-jump defensive and offensive drill (Area 3)	Run-and-jump defensive and offensive drill (Area 4)	Wolf defensive drill (Area 7)	Baby hook shots (Left/right hand) (Baskets 1-6)
19	1	23	Dot shots (Left/right side with no fake) (Baskets 1-2-3)	Dot shots (Left/right side with no fake) (Baskets 4-5-6)	Pivot and pass: Passer (Areas 3 & 4)	Pivot and pass: Passer (Areas 5 & 6)
18	1	24	Dot shots (Left/right side with one fake) (Baskets 1-2-3)	Dot shots (Left/right side with one fake) (Baskets 4-5-6)	Pivot and pass: Defender (Areas 3 & 4)	Pivot and pass: Defender (Areas 5 & 6)

Table 1-1 (cont.)

Score Clock	Duration (Minutes)	Accumulated Time (Minutes)	Varsity Routine Two-Man and Three-Man Groups for the Varsity Players		Junior Varsity Routine Two-Man and Three-Man Groups for the Junior Varsity Players	
			(1A, 1B) (2A, 2B) (3A, 11) [1A, 2A, 3A] [1B, 2B, 11]	(3B, 4A) (4B, 5A) (5B, 12) [4A, 5A, 5B] [3B, 4B, 12]	(1A, 1B) (2A, 2B) (3A, 11) [1A, 2A, 3A] [1B, 2B, 11]	(3B, 4A) (4B, 5A) (5B, 12) [4A, 5A, 5B] [3B, 4B, 12]
17	1	25	Dot shots (Left/right side with two fakes) (Baskets 1-2-3)	Dot shots (Left/right side with two fakes) (Baskets 4-5-6)	Pivot and pass: Pass receiver (Areas 3 & 4)	Pivot and pass: Pass receiver (Areas 5 & 6)
16	3	28	Interception drill (half court)	Interception drill (half court)	Interception drill (half court)	Interception drill (half court)
13	2	30	Setting/receiving screens (Area 3)	Setting/receiving screens (Area 4)	Setting/receiving screens (Area 5)	Setting/receiving screens (Area 6)
11	2	32	Circle box-out drill on shooter (Baskets 1-2-3)	Circle box-out drill on shooter (Baskets 1-2-3)	Circle box-out drill on shooter (Baskets 4-5-6)	Circle box-out drill on shooter (Baskets 4-5-6)
09	2	34	Circle box-out drill on non-shooter (Baskets 1-2-3)	Circle box-out drill on non-shooter (Baskets 1-2-3)	Circle box-out drill on non-shooter (Baskets 4-5-6)	Circle box-out drill on non-shooter (Baskets 4-5-6)
07	1	35	Three-man weave drill (crosscourt)	Three-man weave drill (crosscourt)	Three-man weave drill (crosscourt)	Three-man weave drill (crosscourt)
06	3	38	Long throws for lay-ups drill (crosscourt)	Long throws for lay-ups drill (crosscourt)	Long throws for lay-ups drill (crosscourt)	Long throws for lay-ups drill (crosscourt)
03	3	41	3-on-2 to 2-on-1 drill (crosscourt)	3-on-2 to 2-on-1 drill (crosscourt)	3-on-2 to 2-on-1 drill (crosscourt)	3-on-2 to 2-on-1 drill (crosscourt)
00	0	41	Start of varsity team practice	Start of varsity team practice	Start of junior varsity team practice	Start of junior varsity team practice

Table 1-1 (cont.)

only take two or three minutes to start and complete. The constant transition from one activity to another allows for a great deal of attentiveness and concentration for each and every player.

During the first week of implementation of this routine, the routine can appear to be utter chaos. But, in just a short period of days, the players should learn their routine and the fundamental and stretching period then becomes organized chaos.

Each player will sometimes be in a two-man group, while other times a part of a three-man group, and also occasionally a part of a six-man group. The players in these groups can be set and reset each day for variety and competition. In Table 1-1, two- and three-man groups are denoted as follows: The "A" represents the starting position, and the "B" represents the second-string player at the same position. For example, "1A" is the starting point guard (1), and "1B" represents the second-string point guard (1). The "11" and the "12" are the eleventh and twelfth players of the squad.

This routine could also be implemented in a summer camp format, in pre-season and/or post-season workouts, physical education classes, or at the beginning of in-season practices. The routine could be utilized before every practice during the season or just specific practices.

The entire gymnasium is broken down into specific areas to be utilized for specific drills. Each minute is valuable, and the transition between activities is very important to obtain maximum utilization of time. Diagram 1-1 illustrates the areas/locations for the different drills/activities to be utilized.

The length of each drill is timed on the scoreboard. A whistle or air horn can be used to mark the end of the time period of each drill. One effective way is to have the scoreboard clock set at 42 minutes and turned on at the beginning of the entire routine. A manager can then buzz the horn at the end of each drill/activity to signal the transition from one drill to the next.

Each drill/activity is given a specific location in the gym where that drill should take place. A brief description of each drill/activity will be explained.

The routine starts with 42:00 on the score clock. While the varsity squad is basically spending the first five minutes doing predominantly stretching activities in Areas 1, 2, 3, and 4; the junior varsity squad will be using the two dribbling lines (8 and 9) and all six baskets.

For the next four minutes (with 38:00 on the clock), the varsity will use the six baskets and the areas near those baskets along with Area 7. The junior varsity will use Areas 3, 4, 5, and 6.

With 34:00 on the clock, for one minute, the varsity breaks down with the first six-man squad in Area 7 and the second six-man squad going to an assigned basket. The junior varsity squad uses Areas 3 and 4 for this lone minute.

At 33:00 on the clock, the varsity uses the next three minutes in Areas 3, 4, 5, and 6 to work on pivoting and passing techniques, while the junior varsity breaks down into partners and shares each of the six baskets to work on the various types of dot shots.

At 30:00, the varsity moves to the two dribbling lines to work on two minutes each of dribbling techniques. Then, they move to the six baskets in pairs to work on the

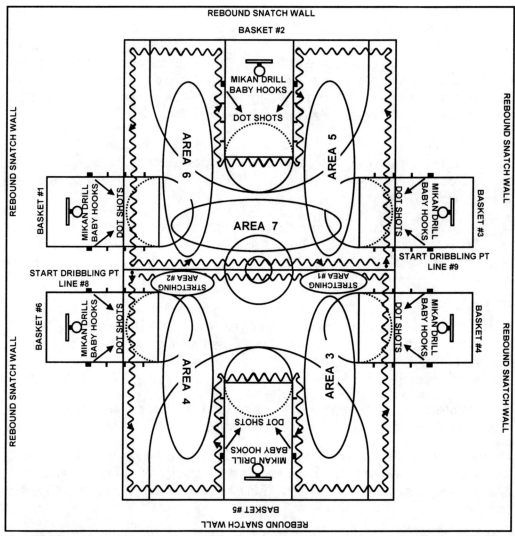

REBOUND SNATCH WALL

BASKET #2

MIKAN DRILL
BABY HOOKS

DOT SHOTS

AREA 6

AREA 5

REBOUND SNATCH WALL

REBOUND SNATCH WALL

BASKET #1

MIKAN DRILL
BABY HOOKS

DOT SHOTS

AREA 7

MIKAN DRILL
BABY HOOKS

DOT SHOTS

BASKET #3

START DRIBBLING PT
LINE #9

START DRIBBLING PT
LINE #8

STRETCHING
AREA #2

STRETCHING
AREA #1

BASKET #6

MIKAN DRILL
BABY HOOKS

DOT SHOTS

DOT SHOTS

MIKAN DRILL
BABY HOOKS

BASKET #4

REBOUND SNATCH WALL

AREA 4

AREA 3

DOT SHOTS

BABY HOOKS

MIKAN DRILL

BASKET #5

REBOUND SNATCH WALL

Diagram 1-1

various power moves to the basket techniques. The junior varsity begins their stretching routine for the next five minutes in Areas 1, 2, 3, and 4.

At 24:00 on the clock, the varsity takes Areas 3, 4, 5, and 6 for five minutes of rebounding and defensive drills. The junior varsity utilizes Area 7 and all six baskets and the wall areas near those baskets for the various shooting and rebounding technique work, in addition to a defensive drill.

At 19:00 on the clock, the varsity uses all six baskets for three minutes to perform the dot shots drill, while the junior varsity uses Areas 3, 4, 5, and 6 to work on the pivot-and-pass techniques.

When the clock runs down to 16:00, both the entire varsity and junior varsity teams group in their respective half courts for three minutes to work on a defensive interception drill. After that, the varsity uses Areas 3 and 4 to work on some offensive screening techniques for two minutes. The junior varsity uses Areas 5 and 6 to do the same.

At 11:00, both the entire varsity and junior varsity teams again group in their respective half-court locations for four minutes on defensive boxing out and offensive rebounding techniques.

At 07:00 on the clock, both teams stay in their respective half-court areas of the main court, to go crosscourt in the so-called full-court drills. When the clock runs down to 0:00, those three drills (which should take seven minutes) are concluded. The entire 42-minute routine is concluded and a positive and enthusiastic tone and attitude has been established for the regular practice for the day.

Shooting Drills

Every shooting drill has specific characteristics that must be emphasized for all players to receive the full benefit from that drill. All shooting drills must be as game-realistic as possible as well as be as time-efficient as possible. Coaches should not want to waste any time during their practice sessions. To make those shooting drills as game-realistic as possible, coaches must incorporate as many types of pressures on the shooters (and the shooters' teammates that are passing the ball to them in the drills) as possible. Coaching staffs should try to incorporate success and competition pressures—trying to beat other players, other squads, other opponents.

The so-called other opponents can be pre-set standards that can vary from player to player. These standards can either be increased or lowered, depending on the circumstances. One opponent that is universal to all players is the clock, and that opponent should be a major part of each shooting drill used.

Coaches should stress accuracy in all of the shooting drills, but should also stress quantity. Stressing quantity of shots will make all players involved in these drills speed up and go at game speed. Coaches should expect all shooters, passers, and rebounders to always go at game speed. Staffs should continually be accelerating their rebounders, passers, and shooters in each and every one of the shooting drills utilized.

A pre-set quantity *and* quality standards set for each shooting drill can be used. Doing so increases the game realism, because each individual is trying to succeed not only for himself, but for his team (or group or squad).

Every shooting drill has a pre-set standard of a specific number of attempts the shooter must take as well as a standard of how many shots the shooter should make. Again, this requirement forces the tempo and intensity level up for each shooting drill that is used.

Game realism also means rewards for the winners and penalties for the players that did not win the competition within the drill. None of the penalties are harsh or hard, but they are a true penalty. They could be some type of a running penalty, some push-ups, or sit-ups that must quickly be done. This form of motivation is used to make each player want to win and never accept losing as acceptable.

Competing against the clock is always beneficial, because everyone has a common opponent. Using the scoreboard clock not only gives everyone a common opponent, but a clear, visible, and constant adversary. Using time limits always speeds up the shooting groups; it does not allow a shooter to take too much time in shooting. Coaches can use Coach John Wooden's invaluable phrase: "Be quick, but don't be in a hurry."

When in a game does a shooter, a passer, or any player have the luxury to take his time and to go at a slower and more comfortable speed? By continually accelerating players in all drills (not just shooting), all players get accustomed to having a much quicker comfortable speed.

Other offensive techniques and fundamentals can be incorporated into each shooting drill, such as passing, rebounding, cutting, coming off screens properly, catching, pivoting, and obviously the shooting. Coaches should study the offenses that are used in games to see where the shots will be manufactured and then incorporate those locations where players will most likely get those shots in games, as well as the types of passes that players will have to use in games.

Coaches should place their passers where they will pass the ball in game situations. Start the shooters in their initial locations, and require the shooters to cut and break to the spots where they most likely will take the shots in games. Require the passers to use the same type of passes they will use in a game, always at game speed. Force the passers to quickly and accurately make the appropriate passes they will make in a game. Sometimes, coaches could have managers have their hands up in front of the shooters to act as dummy defenders, thus making the drill a little more realistic.

Constantly motivate all offensive rebounders to aggressively rebound the basketball before making quick and accurate outlet passes as they would in a real game. If the coach constantly emphasizes the speed and intensity needed, other drills that follow in that day's practice will naturally pick up the same speed and intensity levels that are required for those drills to be successful. Another by-product from these shooting drills can be the conditioning aspect. If everyone works at meeting the quantity and quality standards that have been set, everyone's conditioning will also improve during these drills.

The 55-Second Shooting Drill Format

Many different shooting drills incorporate the 55-second shooting drill theme. Three players are involved in this format. One player is the designated passer, one is the designated shooter, and the last player is the rebounder. The designated shooter must first work on his cutting and breaking to the ball skills so that he may free himself from the hypothetical defender. He then must work on his pass-catching skills and techniques. The all-important pivoting footwork and handwork techniques that will allow him to shoot the ball quickly (but accurately) off the pass are also practiced and utilized in these timed shooting drills. Obviously, the actual shooting skills and techniques are strongly emphasized for the shooter in this three-man drill, but the second player that delivers the ball to the designated shooter also must constantly be cutting and moving without the ball to receive the ball before actually working on the various types of passes he should incorporate to pass the ball to that designated shooter. After catching the ball, this designated passer must apply the proper footwork skills and techniques to make the proper pivot before making the pass to the designated shooter. And, last but not least, the third integral player in all of these 55-second shooting drills is the player that must actually retrieve the made or missed shot. He then must work on his rebounding skills, including the necessary footwork of pivoting to make the outlet pass to the designated passer in this drill. This designated rebounder must learn to read and react to the shooter's shot, gain possession of the offensive rebound, make the appropriate pivot away from his hypothetical defender, and make the proper outlet pass to his teammate. The speed and hustle of the transition of the three players switching their three assignments in this drill is constantly emphasized by the total number of attempted shots that are expected by the three-man group as well as the accuracy of all three players.

After 55 seconds, all three players rotate over one designation, and the drill is repeated. The transition should take no more than five seconds. In three short minutes, each player receives almost one minute (actually 55 seconds) of concentrated work on offensive skills of passing, catching and shooting, rebounding and outlet passing. The rotation is from passer to shooter to rebounder and on to a different shooting location, where the three-man rotation starts again.

Diagram 1-2 displays player 1 (P1) passing to player 2. Player 2 (S2) shoots. Player 3 (R3) rebounds. Diagram 1-3 shows the first rotation. Player 1 is now the shooter. Player 2 becomes the rebounder, and Player 3 rotates to become the next passer.

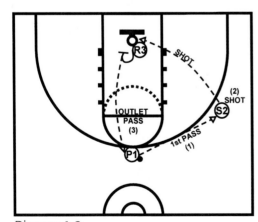

Diagram 1-2

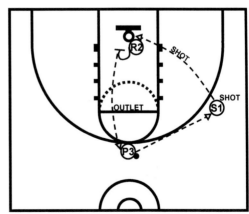

Diagram 1-3

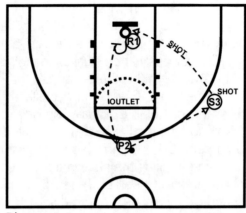

Diagram 1-4

Diagram 1-4 shows the last rotation: Player 1 is the rebounder, player 2 is the passer, and player 3 is the shooter.

   With the rebounder station having to remain near the basket, the locations of the designated shooters and the placement of the designated passers can vary to fit the specific offense's needs. Diagrams 1-5 through 1-9 offer just a few of the many possible combinations of passing and shooting locations. Diagram 1-5 is used to work on the wing shot. Diagram 1-6 is used to practice the skip pass and the shot off of the skip pass. Diagram 1-7 shows the set-up to work on the shot that follows the down pass. Diagram 1-8 demonstrates the action for the up pass. Diagram 1-9 is an example for players to work on the inside shot.

   You could require the shooter to make a move before shooting, especially when drilling on the inside shooting techniques. Different moves could be required each day.

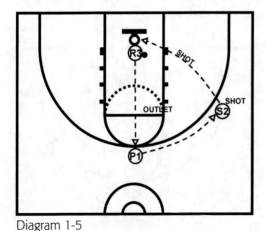

Diagram 1-5

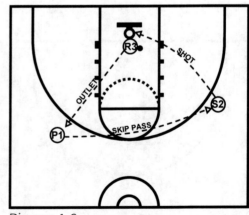

Diagram 1-6

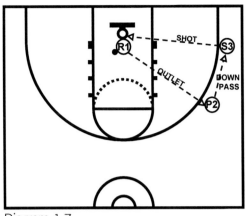

Diagram 1-7

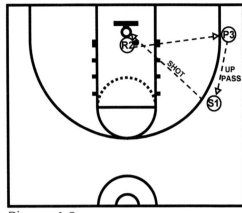

Diagram 1-8

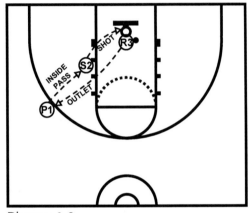

Diagram 1-9

Timed Shooting Drills

In this two-man shooting drill, the passer makes passes from inside the free throw lane to a shooter who is also restricted to a particular area of the court. The areas for the shots could be shots inside the free throw lane (inside shots), outside the free throw lane (outside shots), or behind the three-point line (three-point shots).

The shooter catches the pass and takes a shot as quickly as possible. The passer rebounds the ball, outlet passes the ball back to the shooter for him to continue the drill. After the designated time limit, both players switch roles and assignments. The number of shot attempts and the number of made baskets are counted and recorded for each shooter from each assigned area.

Inside Shots (Diagram 1-10)

A total of three minutes should yield 27 to 30 shots per shooter. A rate of 70 percent accuracy would be about 19 to 21 shots made, 60 percent accuracy would be about 16 to 18 shots made, and 50 percent accuracy would be about 14 to 15 shots made.

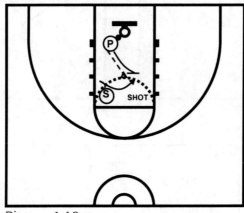

Diagram 1-10

Outside Shots (Diagram 1-11)

A total of three minutes should yield 24 to 27 shots taken per shooter. A rate of 50 percent accuracy would be about 12 to 14 shots made.

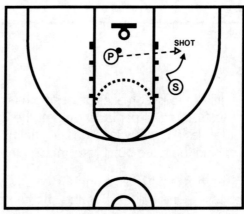

Diagram 1-11

Three-Point Shots (Diagram 1-12)

A total of three minutes should yield 21 to 24 shots taken per shooter. A rate of 50 percent accuracy would be about 10 to 12 shots made.

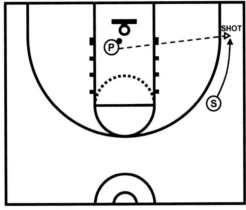

Diagram 1-12

Closeout Shooting Drills off the Pass

The passer (P) makes passes from the free throw lane to a shooter (S) that is also restricted to one of the same three designated areas: inside, outside, or three-point shots areas. The initial passer (P) then follows his pass and closes out on the initial shooter (S), putting token defensive pressure on the shooter. The initial passer remains in that area to become the next shooter. The initial shooter catches the pass (already having his feet and hands ready), takes a shot as quickly as possible, then follows his shot, rebounds the ball, outlet passes the ball back (as the new passer) to the new shooter, and applies token pressure on the new shooter. The two players continue the drill, changing back and forth from being the passer as well as the shooter. The number of attempts and number of made baskets are counted and recorded for each shooter from each assigned area.

The most unique shooting drill in this series has a change in the format of the drill. To increase the quickness and the intensity in the shooting, the rapid fire drill adds a third player and a second basketball. As soon as the first passer makes a pass to a fellow teammate and closes out on him, he instantly becomes the next shooter. The third player in the drill follows the same passing procedures and passes the second basketball to the second shooter. In the meantime, the original shooter has taken his shot, followed the shot for an offensive rebound and then made the outlet pass to the second passer to shoot. The drill can really speed up both the rebounders/passers as well as the shooters and thus increase the intensity level of the drill.

Inside Shots (Diagram 1-13)

A total of three minutes should yield 37 to 39 shots taken for both shooters. A rate of 70 percent accuracy would be about 26 to 27 shots made, 60 percent accuracy would be about 22 to 23 shots made, and 50 percent accuracy would be about 18 to 20 shots made for each shooter.

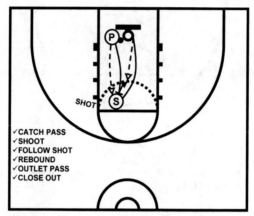

Diagram 1-13

Outside Shots (Diagram 1-14)

A total of three minutes should yield 35 to 37 shots taken for both shooters. A rate of 60 percent accuracy would be about 21 to 22 shots made, 50 percent accuracy would be about 18 shots made for both shooters.

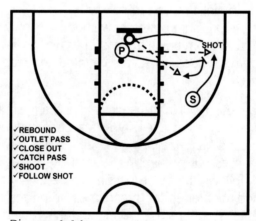

Diagram 1-14

Three-Point Shots (Diagram 1-15)

A total of three minutes should yield 28 to 32 shots taken by both shooters. A rate of 50 percent would be about 14 to 16 made shots for each of the two shooters.

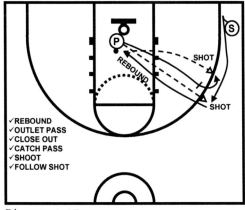

Diagram 1-15

Rapid Fire (Diagram 1-16)

A total of three minutes should yield 26 to 28 shots for each of the three shooters. A rate of 50 percent accuracy would be about 13 to 14 made shots for each shooter. The first passer (01) passes one ball to the first shooter (03) and closes out on that shooter. That shooter (03) takes an outside shot or a three-point shot and follows the shot to become the third passer. As this takes place, the second passer (02) passes a second ball to the first passer (01), who now is the second shooter. The second shooter (01) catches the pass, shoots, and follows his shot to become the fourth passer. The drill continues for the set time limit, with all three players being passers as well as becoming shooters/rebounders.

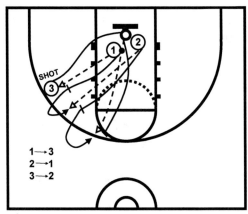

Diagram 1-16

Closeout Shooting Drills off the Dribble

This series of drills is a great complement to the shooting drills. This series adds shot fakes and dribbles for the potential shooter. The passer again makes passes from a specific area to a shooter that is restricted to a particular area. The passer then follows his pass and closes out more quickly on the shooter, putting even more defensive pressure on the shooter. The shooter must then make a realistic shot fake and drive past the defender (scraping off the defender). This drive is directly toward the basket with a predesignated number of dribbles, before then shooting the ball. The driver/shooter should alternate the sides he drives by the token defender. A second shot fake against a second token defender (stationed closer to the basket) may be required before the actual shot at the basket is taken.

The initial passer (P) remains in the area to become the next shooter. The initial shooter (S) catches the pass, takes a shot as quickly as possible, then follows his shot, rebounds the ball, outlet passes the ball back to the new shooter, and applies token pressure on that shooter. The two (or possibly four) players continue the drill, changing back and forth from being passers and defenders to becoming shooters. The number of attempts and number of made baskets are counted and recorded for each shooter from each assigned shooting area. The first sequence in this drill can have all shots taken after the shot fake outside of the free throw lane, while the next sequence can have all shooters taking their shots in the paint. This approach varies the range of shots taken by the squad as well as the amount of close-out defensive pressure on the offensive pass receivers/shooters.

The next sequence of drills in this series adds additional players: one additional teammate and one additional defender. The defender applies varying degrees of pressure on the drivers/passers as well as the shooters. The final shot locations can be varied from in the lane, outside of the lane, and behind the three-point line.

Shot Fake, Drive, and Pull-Up Jump Shot (Diagram 1-17)

Shooters should change the directions they use in attacking the closeout defender and the number of dribbles they use to dribble toward the basket. A total of three minutes should yield 33 to 35 shots attempted by both shooters. A rate of 60 percent accuracy would be about 20 made shots, while 50 percent accuracy would be about 16 to 18 made shots for each shooter.

Shot Fake, Drive, and Power Lay-Up Shot (Diagram 1-18)

The shooter (S) also should fake an outside shot, drive by the closeout defender (D) and take a power shot. He should change the direction he takes in attacking the closeout defender and the number of dribbles used. A total of three minutes should

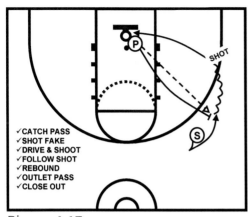

Diagram 1-17

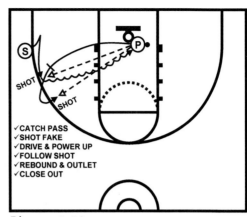

Diagram 1-18

yield 30 to 32 shots taken by both shooters. A rate of 70 percent shooting accuracy would be about 21 to 22 made shots, and 60 percent accuracy would be about 18 to 19 made shots for both shooters.

Shot Fake, Drive, and Power Lay-Up (Diagram 1-19)

Diagram 1-19 depicts the shooter faking then driving only to be picked up by a second defender. The driver then passes off to a teammate for a shot. The shooter (S) must first always make a good shot fake, must always scrape off the closeout defender (P), and then make a power move at the second token defender (D), using between one and three dribbles. The rotation of players could be P to S to D to P. A three-minute total should be about 20 shot attempts for each of the three shooters involved in this drill. A rate of 60 percent would be about 12 shots made by each shooter, and 50 percent accuracy would be about 10 shots made by each shooter.

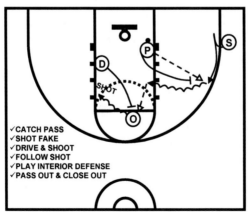

Diagram 1-19

Shot Fake, Dribble Drive, and Dish (Diagram 1-20)

Diagram 1-20 shows the same sequence as Diagram 1-19, except this time the new pass receiver drives to the basket for an inside shot. The shooter (S) first must catch the pass, make a realistic shot fake, and scrape off the closeout defender (D) by taking between one and three dribbles toward the basket. On his subsequent drive to the basket, he should drive and dish to a second offensive player (O), who then takes an inside shot versus the second defender (D), waiting in the lane. A total of four minutes should yield approximately 14 to 16 inside shots for each of the four shooters. A rate of 70 percent accuracy would be about 9 to 11 made shots, and 60 percent accuracy should be about 8 to 10 made shots for each of the four shooters. The rotation of players could be P to S to D to O to P.

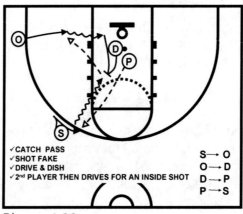

Diagram 1-20

Shot Fake, Dribble, Penetrate, and Pitch (Diagram 1-21)

Diagram 1-21 shows the same sequence as Diagram 1-20, with the new pass receiver shooting a perimeter shot from the deep corner under pressure from the new defender. The shooter (S) first catches the pass from the passer/closeout defender (P) and makes a good shot fake. He takes one to three dribbles toward the basket, but should penetrate and pitch to a second offensive player (O) outside the three-point line, who then takes a three-point shot versus the second defender (D), closing out on him from the lane. The rotation of players could also be P to S to D to O to P. A total of four minutes should yield 10 to 12 shots for each three-point shooter. A rate of 50 percent accuracy would be about five made shots, and 40 percent accuracy would be about four made three-point shots.

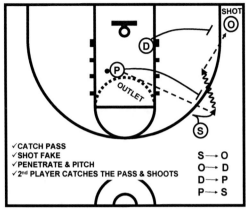

Diagram 1-21

Shot Fake, Dribble Drive, and Pull-Up Jump Shot (Diagram 1-22)

The final drill, shown in Diagram 1-22, can add a second basketball that will increase the tempo of the shooters to make it more game-realistic and get more shots taken in the same time period. The first passer (P1) passes the ball and closes out on the first shooter (S), while the first shooter should shot fake, dribble scrape off the closeout defender, and then drive toward the basket before taking an outside jump shot. The first passer (P1) then becomes the next shooter for the next passer (P2). The rotation of players could be P1 to S to P2 to P1. A total of three minutes should yield about 24 shot attempts for each shooter. A rate of 60 percent accuracy would be about 14 made shots, and 50 percent accuracy would be about 12 made shots for each of the three shooters in this drill.

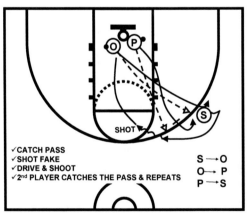

Diagram 1-22

Basic 55-Second Shooting Drills

The basic 55-second shooting drills are shooting drills for groups of three players each. The purpose of these drills is to work on various specific offensive fundamentals at the same time in a game-realistic setting. Offensive rebounding, outlet passing, cutting, catching passes, making passes, and shooting off (receiving) the pass are heavily practiced under the watchful eyes of the coaching staff. All of these techniques can be monitored and observed by the coaches while players can refine those fundamental skills and techniques. Individual players can and should have specific standards they are expected to meet or surpass, as well as the individual three-man groups can also have team/group standards and goals they try to meet or improve on. A great deal of competition is fostered between each individual shooter as well as between each three-man group to help make these drills more game-realistic.

This series of drills has winners and losers. The losing individuals and the losing groups have some form of penalty after the competition is over.

One player in the group starts as the designated rebounder (R), while the next player is assigned the role of the passer, and the third player is assigned the role as the shooter (S). The coaching staff carefully observes each of the three players. Players work on proper techniques of the footwork in their shot preparation, the techniques of shot fakes and drives to the basket, in addition to the actual shooting techniques. The proper fundamental techniques of the actual offensive rebounding and outlet passing, and the proper techniques of passing the ball to the potential shooter also are emphasized and worked on in this multifaceted drill.

Quick transition of each player to their next assignment in the drill is paramount because it saves precious practice time. In addition, the quick transition gives the drill more game realism and, therefore, more value to every player involved. A time clock is always used, with each of the three time frames of the drill lasting 55 seconds for each player to work on the techniques of his specific role. At the conclusion of the 55 seconds is a five-second time frame, when all three players quickly rotate and move to the next role they are to work on. After three rotations, all three players involved have worked on the techniques of: catching and shooting, offensive rebounding and outlet passing, and catching and delivering the ball to the shooter.

Each of the shooter's made shots and attempts are recorded from each of the designated areas. Passers work on the various passes they should make in a game in the positions on the court from which they will make those passes. Shooters work on the various types of shots they will take in a game from the locations of where they will most likely take those shots in game situations. The drill is designed for all players to work in conditions as game-like as possible.

The next sequence involves a bubble defender. The defender in this series of drill can utilize various types of football bubble pads that allow that defender to be more physical with the shooter without causing injury to the shooter. This increase of safe and controlled bumping exponentially makes this series of shooting drills much more game-realistic and gives countless repetitions for the shooter to become more accustomed to the actual physicality of the inside game and increases the shooter's concentration and focus on the actual making of the inside shot. The shooting drills with the bubble defense are drills where all shots are taken in the paint. These physical drills are shooting drills where contact (with the bubbles) is not only allowed but encouraged (within reason). The drill uses one shooter and one rebounder/passer.

In the other drill involving the bubble defense, the two players who are not shooting both have pads, and they both continually harass and make contact with the shooter. The shooter must get his own offensive rebounds and then immediately work on his stickback shots, while the two defenders constantly get in the way of the new offensive rebounder/stickback shooter and continue the controlled physical contact with the offensive player.

Perimeter Shots off the Pass (Diagram 1-23)

All shots are taken off of the pass from the passer, who has received the outlet pass from the rebounder. A total of three minutes should yield about 13 shot attempts for each shooter. A rate of 60 percent accuracy would be about seven to eight made shots, and 50 percent accuracy would be about six to seven made shots.

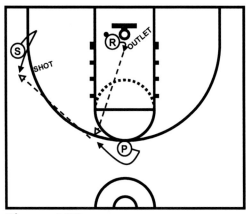

Diagram 1-23

45

Perimeter Shots off Dribble After One Shot Fake (Diagram 1-24)

The shooter should catch the pass, make a realistic shot fake, and take one dribble toward the basket, before pulling up for a jump shot off the dribble. A total of three minutes should yield about 9 to 10 shot attempts for each shooter. A rate of 50 percent accuracy would be about four to five made shots.

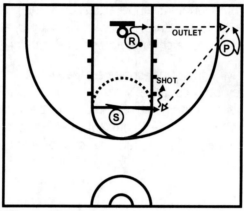

Diagram 1-24

Inside Shots vs. Bubble Defense (Diagram 1-25)

The rebounder/passer/defender (R) should rebound the ball and pass the ball to the shooter (S) and then approach the shooter with his hands up, while the defender (X) has bubble pads and continuously bumps and fouls (again, within reason) the shooter. The rotation of players could be R to S to X to R, after every 55-second time limit. A total of three minutes should yield about 20 inside shot attempts for each shooter against the two defenders in the lane. A rate of 50 percent accuracy would be about 10 made shots per shooter.

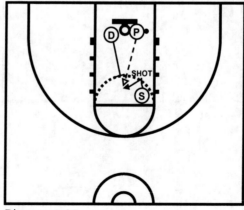

Diagram 1-25

Second Shots vs. Bubble Defense (Diagram 1-26)

The stickback shooter must follow his shot, get his own rebound, and quickly take the second shot for the stickback (against two defenders, both with the football bubble pads). A pump fake before the stickback is encouraged. (A total of three minutes should provide time for each shooter to attempt 22 to 24 inside shots. A rate of 50 percent accuracy would be about 11 to 12 made stickbacks for each shooter.

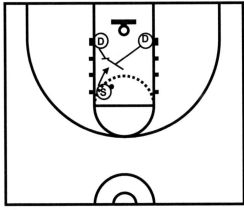

Diagram 1-26

Rapid Fire 55-Second Shooting Drill (Diagram 1-27)

The rapid fire 55-second shooting drills are shooting drills involving three players, with both non-shooters each having a basketball and acting as combination passers/ rebounders. Both retrieve their basketball that the shooter has shot and quickly pass the ball back to the shooter (S). With two basketballs, the shooter must quickly take one shot, then instantly get his feet and hands ready to catch the next pass to quickly shoot again.

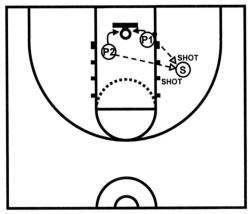

Diagram 1-27

This drill continues for 55 seconds before a new shooter is designated with the remaining two players becoming the rebounders/passers (P1 and P2). This drill is an intense drill that provides a concentrated amount of shooting by each shooting participant of the drill. This drill forces the shooter to get prepared to catch and shoot, quickly recover, and get ready to shoot again. With two basketballs, the shooter should be able to take a much higher number of shots in the 55 seconds of allotted time. After 55 seconds, a new shooter rotates in this high intensity drill. Coaches must closely monitor that the speed of this drill is not counterproductive and start developing bad habits of the shooter.

The three offensive players are described and named as the shooter (S), passer/rebounder (P1), and rebounder/passer (P2). All shots are quickly taken off of the pass, with two players acting as combination of both rebounders and also as passers. Again, this drill must be closely monitored so as not to develop bad habits in the rush of shooting the ball. A total of three minutes should yield 22 to 24 shot attempts for each shooter. A rate of 60 percent accuracy would be about 13 to 14 made shots per shooter, and 50 percent accuracy would be 11 to 12 made shots for each shooter.

Power Shots (Left and Right Sides)

These power shot shooting drills are designed for all players to work on catching the ball in the paint and then applying the post player's power moves against a token post defense. The defender should again utilize the football bubble pads to provide physical play and bump the offensive player as the drill is being run.

This drill can use a designated post player (S), a passer (P), and a defender (X). After two minutes, all three players rotate with the first passer (P) becoming the next post player, the initial post player (S) becoming the new defender (X), and the original defender becoming the next passer. The rotation of the players in this shooting drill is S to X to P. Both sides of the lane should be worked for one minute in their two-minute shooting segment.

Another way of applying these shooting drills for post players is to make it a one-man drill. That one player tosses the ball out in front of himself (as if it were a bounce pass). He (underhand) tosses the ball (to himself), catches and chins the ball, imagines where the imaginary defender is, and makes the appropriate move, dependent upon where the hypothetical post defender is.

As he catches the ball, he should take a small hop and land on both feet at the same time. This move allows him to be able to use either foot as the final pivot foot. Two post players (one on each side of the lane) can operate at the same time from each basket that is available. Their catches, moves, and final shots are staggered so that each player has an unobstructed path to the basket. Again, the shooter goes for a two-minute time period before the drill concludes.

Show-and-Go-Opposite Drop-Step Power Moves (Diagram 1-28)

These moves should be made both toward the middle as well as toward the baseline. Coaches should strongly emphasize that successful offensive post players are players that are unpredictable and can go in either direction and from both blocks. These moves should always start on the first notch above the block on both sides of the lane.

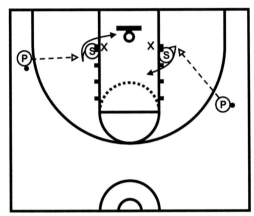

Diagram 1-28

The post player's fakes should be realistic, before the post player actually makes his drop-step move to the basket (in the opposite direction of the fake). A total of two minutes should yield 20 shot attempts for each shooter. A rate of 80 percent accuracy would be 16 made shots, 60 percent accuracy would be 12 made shots, and 50 percent accuracy would be 10 made shots.

Square-Up, Up-and-Under Crossover Power Moves (Diagram 1-29)

These effective post moves should also be made both toward the middle as well as toward the baseline, in order to prevent predictability by the defensive opposition.

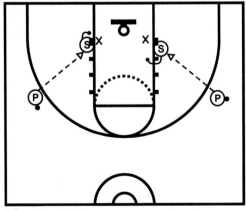

Diagram 1-29

These moves should start on the first notch above the block on both sides of the lane. All post player's shot fakes should be realistic, before the player actually squares up to the basket and then makes his up-and-under move to the basket. These moves should be made both toward the baseline and also toward the middle of the lane (starting from both sides of the lane). A total of two minutes of this drill should yield 18 shot attempts for one post player in his time segment. A rate of 70 percent accuracy would be 12 to 13 made shots for each shooter, while 60 percent accuracy would be 10 to 11 made shots, and 50 percent accuracy would be nine made shots.

Whirl Moves (sometimes called "Olajuwon Moves") (Diagram 1-30)

These spin or whirl moves should be made both toward the baseline as well as toward the middle. These effective scoring post moves should also be initiated from both sides of the lane, so that the post player is not one-dimensional. A total of two minutes should yield 20 shot attempts for the shooter in his shooting time segment. A rate of 80 percent accuracy would be 16 made shots, 60 percent accuracy would be 12 made shots, and 50 percent accuracy would be 10 made shots)

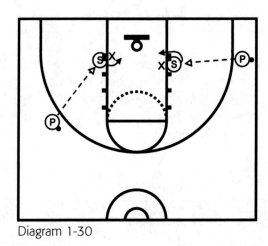

Diagram 1-30

One-Man Dot Shots—With a Shooter, No Defense, No Passer

The three drill series of one-man dot shots can be an invaluable teaching tool for not only post players, but for all offensive players. Because only one player and one ball is involved and because a minimum of two players can utilize each basket at a time, this series is both time- and space-efficient.

Each drill begins with the offensive player tossing the ball out to himself toward the (now imaginary) dotted line in the middle of the free throw lane. From there, the offensive player catches the ball and squares up to the basket with an inside heel pivot. From there, the offensive player is in the middle of the lane and facing the basket with his dribble still intact. He can shoot immediately off the pass, off a shot fake, off the shot fake and dribble, and many other combinations. This drill is an excellent way to develop the footwork of all offensive players both inside as well as on the perimeter. Shot fakes and explosive dribble attacks can also be improved upon by both post players and perimeter players.

The three one-man dot shot drills are:

- *No fakes, no dribble* (Diagram 1-31): A total of two minutes should yield 20 shot attempts. A rate of 70 percent accuracy should be about 14 made shots, and 50 percent accuracy should be about 10 made shots.
- *One fake, one dribble* (Diagram 1-32): A total of two minutes should yield 14 shot attempts. A rate of 70 percent accuracy should be about 9 to 10 made shots, and 50 percent accuracy should be about seven made shots.
- *Two fakes, one or two dribbles* (Diagram 1-33): A total of one minute should yield 12 shot attempts. A rate of 70 percent accuracy should be about seven to eight made shots, and 50 percent accuracy should be about six made shots.

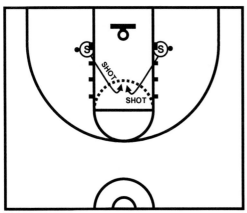
Diagram 1-31

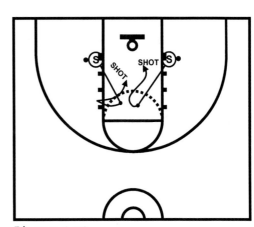
Diagram 1-32

Diagram 1-33

One-Man Close Shots—With a Shooter, No Defense, No Passer

• Mikan Drill—One-Man Drill (Left and Right Sides) (Diagram 1-34)

The Mikan drill is a continuous lay-up drill, with no dribbles involved, using the left and the right hand on the respective sides of the basket. This drill can help all players work on footwork, dexterity, shooting the basketball with both hands, developing a soft touch, and improving on a player's basket education. Without any defense and the close proximity to the basket, a high degree of shooting accuracy should take place, which should improve the shooter's confidence. One minute should yield about 15 shot attempts. A rate of 80 percent accuracy would be about 12 made lay-ups.

• Baby Hook Shots—One-Man Drill (Left and Right Sides) (Diagram 1-35)

The baby hooks drill is simply a progression of the Mikan drill—just two to three feet farther from the basket. It is a continuous, very short hook shot shooting drill, with either one or no dribbles involved, using the left and the right hand on the respective sides of the basket. One minute should yield about 10 to 12 shot attempts. A rate of 80 percent accuracy would be about 8 to 10 made close-to-the-basket hook shots.

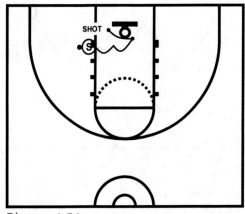 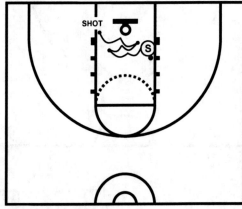

Diagram 1-34   Diagram 1-35

Duck-In Shots With Various Power Moves (Diagram 1-36)

Each offensive shooter should rip-step through the (imaginary) defense and duck in to dotted circle, and then make the various drop-step power moves to the basket. It is a one-man drill with only imaginary defense. Two separate offensive players can work at the same basket—one coming from each of the left and right blocks.

This drill is a continuous power move drill, with one dribble involved, using the appropriate drop-steps toward the baseline, coming from the respective sides of the basket. Dexterity, footwork techniques, and shooting touch are just three of the many techniques and skills that can show immediate improvement in this time-efficient shooting drill. One minute should yield about 12 shot attempts. A rate of 80 percent accuracy would be about 10 made power move shots.

Spin Screen Shots From the Secondary Break—One-Man Drill
(Coming From Both Sides of the Lane) (Diagram 1-37)

This drill can allow each offensive post player the opportunities to work on the preliminary footwork that eventually leads to receiving the (imaginary, in the case of this drill) spin screen before receiving the pass (from the shooter himself, in this drill), and concluding with a drop-step toward the baseline and a power move shot. One minute should yield about 8 to 10 shot attempts. A rate of 80 percent accuracy would be about six to eight made power move shots.

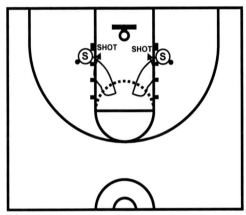

Diagram 1-36

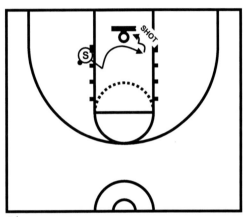

Diagram 1-37

Flex Breakdown Shooting Drill (Diagram 1-38)

This offensive breakdown drill covers an offensive team's passing, cutting, and screening skills, as well as shooting from specific areas on the court. If your team is going to utilize the flex man-to-man offense or any version of the flex, this team shooting drill not only provides the team with countless repetitions of shooting from the locations where the players will take shots in games out of the flex offense, but also it will give each player numerous opportunities to work on the several techniques (other than shooting) that the offense will require in order for it to be successful—such as passing, cutting, catching, and screening. This drill is really a breakdown of the flex offense. If the flex offense is not utilized, whatever man or zone offense that a team is using that season can be dissected and broken down so that the integral parts that include the cutting, screening, dribbling, and pivoting of various offensive players can be "repped" constantly during this drill (or a modification of this drill).

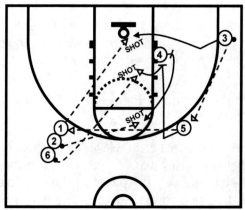

Diagram 1-38

Each possession of this drill requires six players and three basketballs. The first ballside corner (03) up passes to the ballside wing (05), who reverse passes the ball to the weakside wing (01). This move triggers the flex action. The first weakside wing (01) in line receives the reversal pass and then hits the back screen cutter (03), who takes a power shot in the lane. The second (in line) weakside wing (02) passes the ball he already has in his possession to the original back screener (04) who has just received a down screen. 04 takes a jump shot off the pass at the elbow area. The third (in line) weakside wing (06) passes the ball that he started the drill with and hits the original down screener (05) for a power move shot after he has slipped the down screen he has just set for 04.

After the three shots have been taken, the players rotate to different lines at the coaching staff's determination. This drill should be run for three to four minutes and then set up on the opposite side of the court, for the same types of cuts, passes, and shots to be taken on the opposite side of the court.

The flex spot-ups are where the lines are initially set up, except the weakside corner spot-up position. Three passing lines (all from the weakside wing location of the flex offense) have three actual shooters. Three minutes should yield about 21 to 24 different possessions, with three different shots from three different players in each of the possessions.

40 Shooting Contest (Diagram 1-39)

This shooting drill is a 1-on-1 competition drill, based on shooting quickness and shooting accuracy from four different ranges: lay-up range, outside shot range, three-point shooting range, and free throw shooting range. One shooter starts with the jump shots and finishes with the five free throws, while the opposite shooter starts with the free throws and finishes with the jump shots. Points are awarded only for shots made by that shooter. After each shot, the shooter must follow his shot, retrieve the ball, then

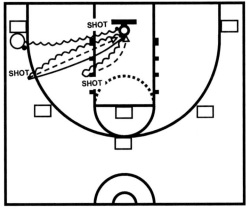

Diagram 1-39

dribble the ball back to the next spot he is to shoot from, and then take the jump shot (or power shot in the lane). The first shooter to finish the drill gets five points, made three-point shots are worth three points each, made two-point jump shots are worth two points apiece, made power shots are worth one point each, and made free throws are worth one point apiece.

The coaching staff should select any five different spots on the court (outside the three-point line). These locations should vary from time to time. The shooter ball fakes and drives for a driving power inside shot (worth one point), then he takes one shot from behind the line (for three points), and he ball fakes and takes an outside shot (for two points). The maximum for each shooting spot on the court is six points if all three jump shots are made (1 + 3 + 2 = 6). At one point in time, each shooter takes five consecutive free throws (each made free throw is worth one point). A perfect score would be 35 points, with an additional five points awarded to the shooter who finishes first. The direction of the fakes and the number of dribbles taken should be designated by the coaching staff and they should change often. This drill should take only three minutes for both shooters to complete.

Beat Michael Jordan Shot Drill (Diagram 1-40)

This shooting drill is for two players, each competing against an imaginary player: Michael Jordan. One shooter starts from the left side, while the other shooter starts from the right side. Each shooter should take 18 various shots apiece—six shots from each of the three ranges of shots. The coaching staff should vary the different spots on the floor. Every shot is taken off a pass to the shooter (by the shooter himself with a short ball toss out) or designated by the coaching staff to be a shot off a designated type and number of dribbles. Every spot has a three-point shot, an outside shot, and an inside shot. The scoring is one point for every made shot, and one point for Jordan for every shot the shooter misses. The shooter's score must beat Michael Jordan's score. A penalty could be assessed for every point below Jordan's score at the end of the

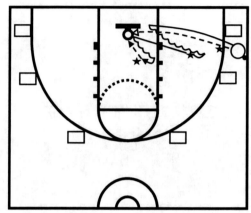

Diagram 1-40

drill. Awards and penalties are assessed to those that beat Jordan and those that lost to Jordan. This drill should take about two to three minutes for each shooter to finish, dependent upon whether dribbles are called for in the drill.

Follow Your Shot Shooting Drill (Diagram 1-41)

This shooting drill is similar to the closeout shooting drills. The three-minute shooting drill starts with two passers underneath the basket. The first passer (01) passes it out to the first shooter (03) and closes out with hands up. The first shooter (03) catches the pass, shoots, and follows his own shot with a stickback (using no dribble, regardless of whether the initial shot was made or missed).

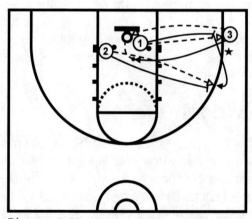

Diagram 1-41

While the first stickback takes place, the first passer (01) squares up and receives a pass from the second passer (02). The second passer (02) repeats the techniques the first passer used, while the first passer (01) repeats what the shooter did. The original shooter (03) then repeats what the second passer (02) did.

The shooting spots can remain the same, or they can be constantly changing. The jump shooter must not only follow his shot, but also take a stickback shot after he has grabbed the offensive rebound. He then makes an outlet pass to his partner in the drill, who has now set up to become the next jump shooter. He makes the outlet pass and closes out on the new jump shooter, who then repeats the routine the original jump shooter has performed.

The accuracy level goals vary for each individual shooter. The outlet pass should not be made until the stickback is being shot. Each shooter should complete 15 repetitions of both shots (jump shot and stickback) during the three minutes of the drill.

Free Throw Swish Shooting Drill (Diagram 1-42)

This shooting drill is simply a free throw shooting contest between groups of four players at each basket. The scoring system requires that players not only make the free throws, but make the free throw in a much tougher way. Free throw shooters only count the free throws shot when they actually swish the shot, which forces each shooter to concentrate even more. Each shooter must shoot five pairs of free throws and must also keep score of his shooting accuracy. With four players at each basket, only three baskets are needed for an entire team of 12 players. The scoring just for this shooting drill is kept in the following manner:

- A swished free throw is a free throw that is made and touches nothing but net. That swished free throw is worth two points.
- A made free throw (that is not swished) is worth one point, while a missed free throw is worth zero points.
- This drill should take five minutes for all four shooters (in each of the three groups) to each shoot five pairs (10 actual free throws) of shots. Small penalties could be given to the fourth-, third-, and second-place finishers. A high-energy drill that requires running should be used immediately before utilizing this drill to make sure the free throw shooters are fatigued and winded prior to shooting the free throws (to make the free throw shooting more game-realistic).

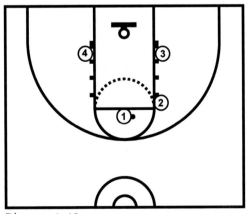

Diagram 1-42

Solo Shooting Drill (Diagram 1-43)

This solo shooting drill is a competition between each individual player on the squad relying solely on himself. After each shot, the shooter must hustle to retrieve the ball. He does not take a stickback shot in this shooting drill, but instead quickly dribbles back to the perimeter to take his next perimeter shot. He then repeats the shot, the following of the shot, and the dribbling out to the same location. He must dribble quickly with his head up so that he does not interfere with one of the other players shooting at the same basket. The coaching staff should designate the locations from which the shooters are to shoot. The coaching staff should also determine whether the shooters pass the ball to themselves (so that the shooter must shoot the jump shot directly and immediately off the pass) or allow the shooter to take one dribble and shoot off the dribble. The squad can be broken up into equally divided groups for each basket available, with a maximum of five shooters at each basket and one ball per man.

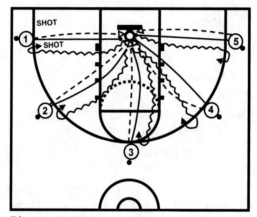

Diagram 1-43

The coaching staff designates penalties for the losing individuals. Each shooter must keep track of his made jump shots and call out his new score after every made jumper. After each 25 seconds, the shooters must rotate to the next location to his right. 01 moves to 02's spot, while 02 moves to 03's spot, 03 moves to 04's spot, 04 moves to 05's spot, and 05 moves to 01's original spot. This transition should take no more than five seconds, and the drill restarts for another 25 seconds. The 25-second shooting period is for each of the shooting spots. A subtle by-product of this drill is each player improves on the habit of following his shot, his dribbling skills, and even a degree of physical conditioning with a maximum of three minutes per each time the drill is executed.

Each player shoots a jump shot and follows his shot to retrieve the ball. He then dribbles out to that same spot on the same side of the floor to take the next jump shot off of the dribble or after a pass to himself. The goal is to take six to eight shots per minute. Every shooter then rotates to the next spot to repeat the drill at a different spot.

The drill should take five minutes for each shooter to shoot at all five designated spots, with each shooter taking about 30 to 40 shots.

Team Bonus Free Throw Shot Drill

This free throw shooting drill is a shooting drill that puts pressure on each free throw shooter to not make one free throw, but to make two free throws in a row. The first free throw is of the most importance: only a made free throw allows the shooter to have the opportunity to take the second free throw shot. This drill is game-realistic, because it is identical to an actual game's bonus free throw situation.

If the shooter misses either of the free throws, the whole team faces some type of running penalty. Immediately after the running, the next player then steps to the line to attempt to make the one-and-one free throw simulation.

Free Throw Shooting Drill (12 Balls, 12 Men) (Diagram 1-44)

Each player shoots a one-and-one bonus free throw. If the shot is made, that shooter gets another free throw attempt. If the shooter misses the front end of the one-and-one, the entire team has a full sprint to run. If the shooter makes the front end and then misses the second free throw, the team has to run half of a full sprint. If the shooter makes both ends of the one-and-one, the team has no running to do. After all team members have completed the first phase, a second and possible third phase could be performed (with the running penalties stepped up in length for each additional shooting phase). Each phase should take approximately 2.5 to 3.5 minutes apiece.

Team Pressure Free Throw Shooting Drill (Diagram 1-45)

A specified number of free throws must be made (determined by the coaching staff). An example would be for a 12-man team to make 20 free throws in the one circuit. This drill should take about 2.5 to 3.5 minutes for all 12 players to shoot the one-and-one.

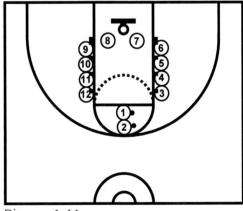

Diagram 1-44

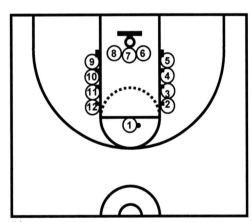

Diagram 1-45

Tennessee Free Throw Shooting Drill (Diagrams 1-46 through 1-49)

This outstanding drill incorporates many different offensive and defensive skills and techniques in a small period of time. It is very game-realistic and has competition, game speed, and pressures. The drill is very time- and space-efficient. The drill incorporates shooting, passing, cutting, offensive rebounding, defensive boxing out, and defensive rebounding skills. The drill can be utilized several times in a practice as a way to have a break in the action.

This drill is run in groups of three. Player 01 takes five pairs of free throws, two at a time. A teammate (02) works on offensive rebounding techniques. The other teammate (03) works on his defensive rebounding techniques.

The offensive rebounder (02) lines up next to the defensive rebounder (03) and works on his techniques of beating the defensive box-out for the offensive rebound. If he does get the rebound, he must quickly power up the stickback. The defensive rebounder (03) lines up in the appropriate position in the free throw lane and works on boxing out the offensive rebounder (02).

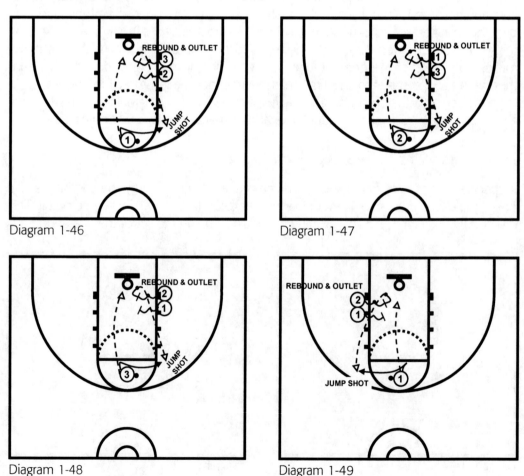

Diagram 1-46

Diagram 1-47

Diagram 1-48

Diagram 1-49

If (03) gets the defensive rebound off the missed free throw, he quickly makes the outlet pass to the free throw shooter (01). 01 has rotated to the elbow position for a quick jump shot. After the second free throw is shot, the rebounder (made free throw or missed) quickly makes an outlet pass to that free throw shooter. 01 takes a jump shot from the elbow area.

After the jump shot, all three players rotate to a different position for the next pair of free throws. The free throw shooter rotates to become the new defensive rebounder, the defensive rebounder moves to become the new offensive rebounding station, and the offensive rebounder moves to become the next free throw shooter.

Diagram 1-46 displays the original group. Diagram 1-47 shows the first rotation. Diagram 1-48 depicts the second rotation. Diagram 1-49 shows the original shots from the opposite side of the court.

After all players have taken their five pair of free throws, they report their scores to a manager who keeps statistics. Each player should have a designated number of free throws he is supposed to make. Awards and penalties are assigned to each individual free throw shooter.

A total number of free throws must be made for each session. That number is predetermined. Team awards and/or penalties are given to the team for total free throws made. The team knows the number before the shooting begins.

Awards can be given for a predetermined number of offensive rebounds. The team knows this number. Penalties are assets for each defensive rebounder who allowed an offensive rebound.

Four goals and basketballs are needed for this drill to have four groups of three players. This drill is more game-realistic when the coaching staff has some type of strenuous activity from either full-court or half-court immediately preceding the Tennessee free throw drill.

The next time this drill is run, the two rebounders should stack up on the opposite side of the free throw lane, so that both sides are equally utilized. The drill provides opportunities for all three players to shoot their five pairs of free throws, to take between five and 10 jump shots, to defensively box out 10 times, to make between five and 10 defensive rebounds followed by outlet passes, and to make between five and 10 offensive rebounds.

Offensive Pivoting and Passing Breakdown Drills

This important drill is included in the pre-practice fundamental and stretching routine. Because it is such a time-efficient drill and because it encompasses so many different fundamentals, this drill should be utilized in practice sessions more than once each practice.

The pass receivers (03, 06, 09, and 012 in Diagram 1-50) work first on the pre-catch and pre-shooting stance. The coaching staff constantly is emphasizing for the (potential) Shooter to get his feet and hands ready, to get behind the ball, and to give the passer a target. Even before the catch of the basketball, the pass receiver already has his inside shoulder (shoulder closest to the basket) facing the basket, and has his guide hand up as if he is already shooting the ball. The shooting hand is also in the position as if the shooter has already caught the ball and is about to shoot. With the shooting hand in that position, the pass receiver can easily give a target to the passer. You can tell your players that is similar to a catcher in baseball giving the pitcher a target to pitch to, making that pitcher (passer in this case) a better pitcher (passer.) A better pass makes it easier for the shooter to get a good shot. In addition, the pass receiver should always pivot off the heel of his inside foot (the foot closest to the basket).

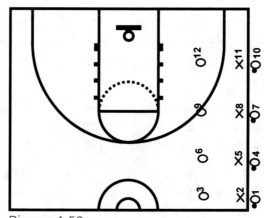

Diagram 1-50

If the pass receiver is in a stationary position, he can start with the inside heel already touching the floor and the remaining portion of that foot not yet touching the floor. If the pass receiver is on the move, he might have to chop up his steps in order to time the inside heel hitting the floor (to pivot) just as the ball hits the palm of the shooting hand. From there, the heel being planted first will stop the pass receiver's forward momentum off his cut toward the passer.

The shooter should be able to rise straight up and come back straight down. Shooters should not to be floating in either direction. Stopping all of the momentum from the shooter's cut before he shoots the ball will make the shooter a much more accurate shooter.

Once the momentum is stopped, the heel actually will allow for a smooth, easy and, complete pivot toward the basket. The shooter swings his free (outside) foot and leg around so that he is completely squared up to the basket.

In this particular drill, the pass receiver/shooter shoots the ball back to the original passer. The passer is quickly ready to resume working on his technique of passing to the shooter. The shooter quickly works on the foot and handwork part of his shooting technique.

The men in the middle of the drill (X2, X5, X8, and X11 in Diagram 1-50) are defenders. They initially guard the dribbler/passer. These defenders work on proper stances and other defensive fundamentals. The defensive player works on defensive techniques only on the original dribbler/passer, not on the shooter.

The dribbler/passers (01, 04, 07, and 010 in Diagram 1-50) work on the dribbling, pivoting, and passing techniques and skills. The first technique to be worked on is the dribble as the dribbler approaches the defender. Dribbling quickly (but in a very controlled manner) with the head up in a semi-crouch stance is the first point of emphasis for the offensive player. Practicing using both hands to dribble and the use of the primary passing hand is the second major point of emphasis.

The next technique to master is the pivot-and-pass technique:

- Step 1: The Two-Foot Jump Stop (Diagram 1-51). As the dribbler approaches the defender and kills his dribble, have the dribbler take a small bunny hop and land simultaneously on both feet. This move allows the killed dribbler to use either foot as the pivot foot.
- Step 2: The Step-Out (Diagram 1-52). If the passer wants to attack the defender by passing laterally around the defender's left side, the dribbler should land and make his left foot his pivot foot. This move makes the passer's right foot his free foot, the foot that can laterally step toward the outside of the defender's left foot. As this is taking place, the passer should protect the ball by firmly holding the ball with both hands. The ball is held beside the knee of the free foot (the right knee, in this example). If the passer's free foot is laterally outside the defender's foot, the passer then could fake low and go high, or fake high and go low (passing over or under the defender's left hand). Constantly tell the dribbler-turned-passer to protect the ball beside the knee and to step due east or due west.
- Step 3: The Rip-Through (Diagram 1-53). If the defender counters the dribbler's first lateral attack, the dribbler rips the ball low and hard across the shoe tops as he steps with a front pivot across the face of the defender. This move allows the dribbler/passer to laterally attack the defender on the opposite side (in this scenario, it is the defender's right side). The ball ends up on the inside of the knee of the passer's free leg (the right knee, in the diagram). If the passer's free foot (right) gets outside defender's right foot, the passer looks to pass the ball around the defender (fake high and go low, or fake low and go high) on the opposite side from the initial side of attack. Again, strongly emphasize to the pivoting passer to protect the ball beside the free knee (right) and to step due east and/or due west in the lateral attacks on the ball defender.
- Step 4: The Swing-Around (Diagram 1-54). If the ball defender reacts quickly and takes this second method of passing away, coaches should emphasize to the offensive player to remain in the semi-crouch stance, then quickly reverse pivot off

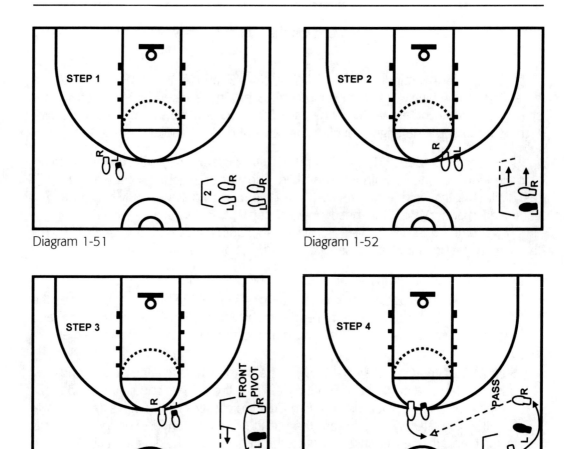

Diagram 1-51

Diagram 1-52

Diagram 1-53

Diagram 1-54

the same (left) pivot foot and attack the ball defender's original (left) lateral side. The ball should now be back beside the knee of the free (right) foot. Again, the main three points of emphasis to the passer are:

✓ Protect the basketball by placing the ball beside the free knee,

✓ Step outside the defender's foot (outflank the defense by going east or west),

✓ Fake a pass to make a pass, or fake high and go (pass) low or fake low and go (pass) high.

If the defense counters this third step, the dribbler should reverse pivot (away from the defender) and look to make an uncontested pass to another teammate or attempt to use the same previous three steps again.

After 55 seconds, the dribbling/pivoting/passing player (01) switches to the defensive station, the first defender (X2) switches to work at the pass receiving/shooting station, and the first pass receiver/shooter (O3) rotates to the dribbling/pivoting/passing station. This rotation should take less than five seconds, and the drill starts again.

After the third 55-second time frame has concluded, start the second round with all offensive dribblers using the right foot as the pivot foot. In just six minutes, three players have each had almost two minutes of concentrated work on all three stations: the dribbling, pivoting, and passing phase, the defensive phase, and the pass catching and shooting phase.

Offensive Rebounding Drills

Circle Box-Out Drill (Diagram 1-55)

The circle box-out drill is an offensive and defensive rebounding drill using a circle to aid in correcting footwork required for either making successful defensive box-outs or in defeating the opposition's defensive box-outs and getting to the ball to offensive rebound. By using a circle, the coach can easily see when footwork is not properly executed and to check to see if the defense has prevented the offensive rebounder from advancing toward the ball.

Start this important drill by placing a basketball in the center of the jump circle at mid-court with a defender facing out opposite the ball and with his heels on the outer edge of the circle. Align the offensive rebounder a full step from (and to the outside of) the defender. When the coach yells "Shot," the defender works on the various methods of boxing out the offensive rebounder. The offensive rebounder works on his techniques of defeating the defensive box-out.

The drill is a 1-on-1 competitive drill with a winner and a loser. If the offensive rebounder can grab or at least touch the basketball within a three-second count after the imaginary shot is taken, he is the winner. If the defender prevents the offensive rebounder from making contact with the basketball within the three-second time limit, the defense wins.

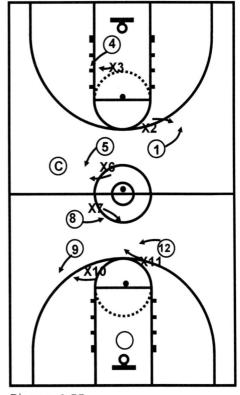

Diagram 1-55

The three varying scenarios where both the offensive players and the defensive players develop their appropriate techniques are as follows:

- The offensive player acts like he is the actual shooter (04 and 01 in Diagram 1-55).
- The offensive player is just one pass away (05 and 08 in Diagram 1-55) from the imaginary passer/shooter.
- The offensive player is more than one pass away (09 and 12 in Diagram 1-55) from an (imaginary) offensive player who is on the either side of the circle and takes the (imaginary) shot when the coach yells "Shot!"

The offensive rebounder can use three techniques. All three of these important offensive techniques can be used in any of the three shooting scenarios:

- As the defense makes contact with the offensive rebounder, the offensive rebounder can go butt-to-butt and spin off (the defender) and continue after the basketball.
- The offensive rebounder can use a swim technique to escape the contact of the defensive box out before hustling to the ball.
- The offensive rebounder can step backward away from the defensive contact and then slash to the ball, after scraping off the defender. That offensive rebounder should attack the side of the defender who is opposite the side that the defender turns his head to look for the offensive rebounder, when the contact is broken. For example, if the offensive rebounder breaks contact with the defender and the defender turns to look over his right shoulder to visibly find the offensive rebounder, the offensive rebounder should then attack the left side of the defender and slash to the ball.

In just a few minutes, both the offensive and defensive players can have several repetitions. In addition to the center jump circle, each basket that has a free throw line and a top of the key can be a station for the circle box-out drill. With a maximum of two pairs of players at each station and with seven potential stations, 28 different players can be involved.

Defensive Shell Drill (Diagrams 1-56 and 1-57)

The defensive shell drill can be used as an offensive and defensive rebounding drill. The defense allows perimeter players to pass the ball around to each other. After a specific number of passes, the defense should then allow a player to shoot the basketball. With the drill having different shooters from different locations, the defensive scenarios would obviously vary. This variation causes both the defensive players as well as the offensive players to work on rebounding the basketball first using the defensive boxing out techniques on not only the shooter, but the offensive opponent that is one pass away from the shooter, and the opponents that are more than one pass away from the shooter.

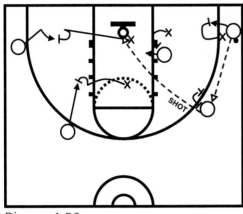

Diagram 1-56

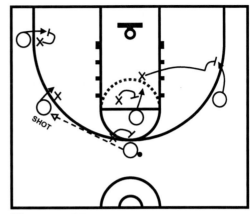

Diagram 1-57

Defensively, have the defenders practice the specific techniques that they should use during the defensive box-outs in a game. Offensively, the coaching staff should have those players work on locating the basketball as it is shot, then to try to determine where the ball would land after the ball has hit the rim or backboard, and then try to get to that location after beating the defensive box-out. Players can rotate from the various locations on the court, both sides of the floor as well as above and below the free throw line extended. After several shots, the players change from offense to defense. In that way, all players become well-rounded both as offensive rebounders as well as defensive players.

Diagram 1-56 displays a pass from a corner player to a wing where the shot is taken. Note the defenders who are one pass from the ball, two passes from the ball, and the defender on the ball. Each defender uses a different defensive technique. But offensive rebounders use one of the three techniques previously described. Diagram 1-57 shows a pass from the point to a wing. The passes could be around the horn instead of just one pass. The defensive rebounders and the offensive rebounders must constantly reevaluate their positioning.

Transition Drills

Super Transition Drill

The primary purpose of this drill is to work on your team's transition game, whether it is from offense to defense or from defense to offense. In essence, Squad A must compete against two different squads, with each of those squads having distinct position advantages over them. By using the overload theory, Squad A going against two squads, the drill makes it extremely difficult for Squad A to execute. Having the drill tougher than actual game situations should improve their performances during games.

The drill is initiated with a 5-on-5 controlled scrimmage. Squad A will be running through their offensive entries or offensive continuities against a defensive group that can be called Squad B. Squad A could devote time and effort on improving their transition from offense to defense after losing possession of the basketball, via (purposely) committing turnovers, missing shots, or actually making shots.

Squad C has absolutely no defensive responsibilities and is stationed in a random manner out near the 10-second line and close to the frontcourt hash marks. Their primary responsibility is to be able to generate a fast break in a much quicker manner than in an ordinary setting, since they have a position advantage to be able to have a head start. This set-up puts extra pressure on Squad A by overloading their degree of difficulty in getting back on defense (with their new offensive opponent having a head start in their offensive fast break).

Defensive Transition After a Turnover
(Diagram 1-58)

The first scenario discusses the defensive transition after a turnover. The offensive team (Squad A) runs an entry or a continuity pattern. On the coaching staff's whistle, the offense could drop the ball (as in a turnover). The defensive team (Squad B) then recovers the loose ball and immediately outlets the ball to an assistant coach, who is located near one of the two frontcourt hash marks. The coach hands the ball to C1, who initiates his team's (Team C) fast break at the other end of the court. C1 must come back and receive the handoff and must then dribble the ball all the way to the opposite end of the court, where his teammates have sprinted ahead to run their primary and secondary fast break. Team C has a head start advantage over all the members of Team A. Team A must sprint back and prevent uncontested shots generated from Team C's fast breaks.

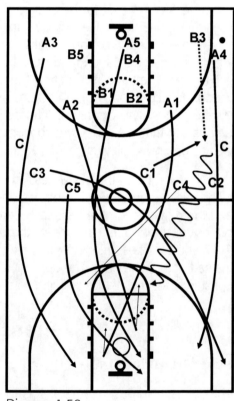

Diagram 1-58

Defensive Transition After a Missed (or Made) Shot (Diagrams 1-59 and 1-60)

The second scenario comes after a made or missed shot. When Squad A takes a shot, they then look to legitimately offensive rebound the missed shot. To maximize the chance for defensive rebounds, you might dictate to Squad A's offensive rebounders to make the effort to rebound, but not allow them to actually grab the offensive rebound. Therefore, all missed shots would result in defensive rebounds by Squad B's defensive rebounders. After securing the defensive rebound, Squad B's rebounders could pitch the outlet pass again out to C1 so that Squad C could run their offensive fast break (with another head start over Squad A). If Squad A actually makes the shot, the assistant coach on the side of the court could use a new basketball and quickly outlet the ball to C1 again to start an immediate fast break for Squad C, going downcourt in the opposite direction.

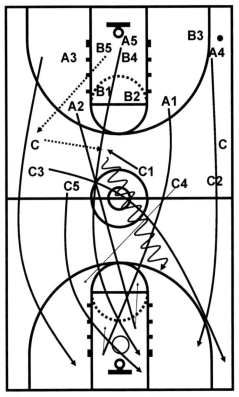

Diagram 1-59

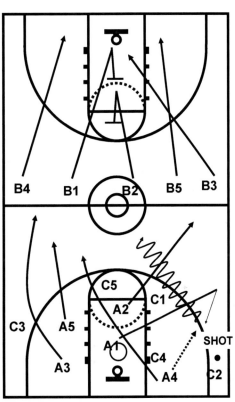

Diagram 1-60

To make it much more difficult for Squad A to get back on defense, Squad C could position themselves and be spread out in a manner that they would have a significant position advantage on Squad A (Diagram 1-59). Obviously, Squad C would have a head start as they sprint out and look for the outlet pass from the assistant coach. The assistant coach pitches the ball out to one of the fast breakers on Squad C, and that group looks to run their primary fast break (and on into their secondary fast break). Squad A must quickly sprint back from offense to defense (after their missed shot) to once again defend their basket against the offensive fast breaking Squad C.

The members of Squad A must sprint back in their defensive fast break lanes as fast as they can to first stop the primary fast break (and ultimately the opponent's secondary fast break) of Squad C.

This new offensive fast break group of Squad C could be instructed to do any one of the following:

- Force a shot out of the primary break or the secondary fast break.
- Force a pass that could most likely become a turnover.
- Remain patient and under control in the offense and look to carefully score in a legitimate manner.

Squad A would initially be working on attempting to prevent easy shots out of the opponents' primary or secondary fast break. Ultimately, when Squad A is on defense and finally regains possession of the ball, they quickly reverse their direction and sprint back (from defense) to offense toward their original basket (Diagram 1-60). Squad A will not have any supplemental group to aid them in transition, so they will again run the entire length of the floor back to their offensive end. Squad A should then execute both their own primary and secondary fast breaks against Squad B. Squad B (the original defensive group) has gained their advantage by moving toward the 10-second timeline, while Squad C has attacked Squad A.

Squad B (converting back on defense) will easily and always get back ahead of Squad A (who is transitioning from defense to offense). Squad A now is forced to execute both their primary and secondary break, as well as possibly into their continuity offense.

As Squad A offensively attacks Squad B, the supplemental group, Squad C positions itself ready to run another offensive fast break. The cycle is ready to be repeated. Both the B and the C squads start with position advantages and also enjoy a breather, while the other squad is competing against Squad A, but Squad A never has a position advantage on anyone and also never has a breather. Squad A competes against both squads. This overload method places Squad A into more difficult situations than they will encounter in a game. Players should be substituted onto Squad A as the drill continues.

Many benefits are to be found in this drill for each of the three groups. Squad A will receive work and practice in the following:

- Running a half-court offense
- Reacting and getting back on defense after turnovers or made/missed shots to prevent easy lay-ups by their defensive opponents
- Reacting quickly to run their own primary and secondary fast breaks on offense (from a half-court defensive setting)
- A great deal of full-court conditioning as they work on the different aspects of their transition game

Squad B will be able to work on their half-court defense as well as the back part of their defense versus an opponent's fast breaks (in a controlled setting). Squad C could be a less talented team (junior varsity or a freshmen team) that could work on a little of their primary break as well as their secondary break.

Squad A and Squad B could easily exchange their original positions so that Squad B could then receive the most attention and work on their own transition game—both offensively as well as defensively.

This drill requires the full court and a minimum of at least 15 participants with each squad having the ability to easily and quickly substitute others into the drill. Three different coaches could actually be coaching each of the three squads with all three coaches having different points of emphasis.

The primary focus of the drill will be devoted to Squad A; therefore, that group would have the largest number of coaching points of emphasis. Of the many focal points, some of the most important are:

- Making sure the tailback (TB), the halfback (HB), and the three fullbacks (FBs) get in the proper positions after the offense has shot the ball. The tailback is descriptively called the safety. He is the assigned offensive player who has full defensive transition responsibilities with no offensive rebounding responsibilities. His job simply is to get his tail back on defense. The offensive player called the halfback is the player designated to be both the half-rebounder and half-safety; half of his job is to get back on defense, and half of his job is to help out somewhat on the offensive boards. His job is the one job out of the five players' jobs that can have adjustments. The three remaining offensive players are the players who have one responsibility and that is to offensive rebound the basketball. These three players are called the fullbacks; their full responsibility is to rebound their team's missed shots.
- Making sure that all five players sprint back in their defensive fast break lanes while looking over their inside shoulder. Running the lanes can clog up and congest the opposition's offensive fast break lanes. Looking over their inside shoulder might allow them to run into an intercepted fast break pass. Once the tailback and the halfback get back to their defensive top of the key, they should then set up defensively in the lane, before building the defense from the inside-out.
- Making sure that either the tailback or the halfback becomes the ball man (B2 in Diagram 1-60), while the other becomes the basket man (B1 in Diagram 1-60).
- Making sure that the ball man and the basket man use the proper procedures and techniques to defend the basket and buy their three defensive teammates some time in getting back.
- Making sure that all five players then get out quickly and run the proper lanes while offensively executing their own primary and secondary fast breaks and on into their half-court offenses.

Among the many advantages to using this drill in practice, the major advantages are a select group of players (Squad A) can be closely scrutinized and taught efficiently in a relative small amount of time. This group can prepare in very real, game-like situations. The only part of the drill that does not resemble game-like situations is the part of the drill that provides an overload theory, making it more difficult than it could possibly be in an actual game.

A concentrated effort can be made by coaches to work with individuals in that selected group. Transition from offense to defense as well as from defense to offense can be worked on a great deal. Half-court offense and defense of any of the three groups participating can be evaluated as well. The physical conditioning of the players of that selected group will be improved. Players can easily be inserted into the particular group to be put under the microscope of the coaching staff.

This super transition drill can be an extraordinary drill in that it can be extremely time-efficient, thus allowing more time in your practices for working on other facets of the game. The overload method of working one particular team against tougher than game conditions makes the drill an invaluable teaching and learning drill, a practice drill as well as a conditioning drill.

Besides offenses and defenses being worked on, the all-important part of the game—called transition—becomes the focal point of the drill. During this drill, many offensive concepts and philosophies can be taught, reviewed, drilled, observed, evaluated, critiqued, and corrected with the players. Likewise, many defensive facets of the game can be practiced with a different group of players at the same time. During the utilization of this drill, a great number of players will be able to watch, listen, learn, participate, and practice in the performance of the drill. The drill will not be boring. No player should have to or be allowed to stand around while the drill is being run. It is also an excellent method of unobtrusively conditioning your players as they are learning and improving many different aspects of their game. It allows a large number of coaches to coach and an even greater number of players to learn, all the while being in the same setting.

3-on-2 to 2-on-1 Transition Drill (Offense and Defense)

This breakdown transition drill is primarily for the two most important players in a team's defensive transition. All players should work on these two defensive positions because any (offensive to defensive) player can end up in one of these two specific positions. While not disregarding the other players, the two players that should be the main focal points of the coaching staff's attention are the two offensive players who will quickly become the first two defenders getting back from offensive to defensive transition. They are called the basket man and the ball man.

If an offensive team misses their shot and surrenders the defensive rebound, two assignments are made for the first two defenders who get back on defense. If the offensive team loses possession of the ball via a turnover, no definite defensive transition assignments are given. It is imperative that the (original) offensive team's basket is immediately protected, regardless of what players get back first. In this case, any of the five players could become the basket man and the ball man.

As in the majority of the drills, coaches should try to make the drills as game-realistic, as competitive, and as time-efficient as possible. So, it is a good idea to incorporate some offensive concepts and philosophies for one group of players to work on as another group works on developing specific defensive skills, all within the framework of the same drill.

3-on-2 Portion of the Drill (Diagrams 1-61 through 1-65)

Two defensive players (X1 and X2) start the drill by literally being seated near the offense's sideline hash mark, and three offensive players (01, 02, and 03) start on the offense's baseline (Diagram 1-61). The ball is advanced via dribbling and/or passing with the three offensive players staying in their three wide lanes. The two defenders must quickly scramble to their feet and then sprint back to defend their basket. The first defender to get back should run to the middle of the free throw lane and call out "Basket," while the second defender to get back should call out, "Ball."

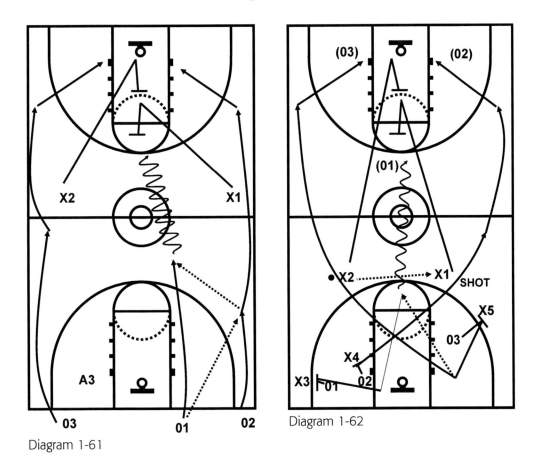

Diagram 1-61

Diagram 1-62

Another method of starting the drill is to have the three offensive players (01, 02, and 03) start in a 3-on-3 defensive alignment against three other players (X3, X4, and X5), with the original two (potential) defenders (X1 and X2) making one or two passes before they shoot and miss to cause a defensive rebound (Diagram 1-62).

The original three defenders (soon to become offensive players 01, 02, and 03) work on boxing out, securing the rebound, and running a three-man fast break in the three lanes. The two original offensive players (X1 and X2) sprint back as quickly as possible, communicating loudly on who is to become ball man and who is going to become basket man. The dummy offensive players (X3, X4, and X5) step off the court and get ready to step into the roles that 01, 02, and 03 are currently playing.

The first defender (X2 in Diagram 1-62) settles in near the dotted circle in the middle of the lane and yells, "Basket!" The second defender settles in the lane (X1 in Diagram 1-62) and approaches the dribbler as far out as the top of the key. He yells, "Ball!"

The ball man (X1) stops the dribble penetration of the dribbler, while the basket man (X2) protects the blocks and takes both the first and second perimeter passes. When the offensive team passes the ball to either wing, the basket man (X2) rotates out to defend the ball (Diagram 1-63). As this is taking place, the original ball man (X1) drops quickly down the lane to protect the basket.

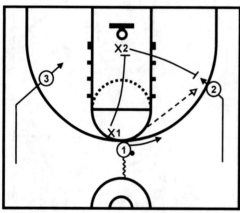

Diagram 1-63

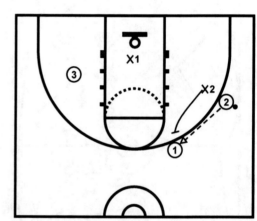

Diagram 1-64

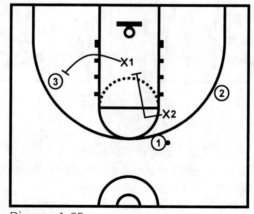

Diagram 1-65

If the ball is passed from the wing back to the point, the original basket man (X2), who has defended the first wing pass, would then defend the reversal pass also. This technique allows the original ball man (X1), who has dropped down to protect the basket, to remain low to continue protecting the basket and the original basket man (X2) to take the first wing pass as well as the next reversal pass (Diagram 1-64). To explain the rotation and the coverage in a simple manner, coaching staffs could use the statement, "The ball man must stop the ball and drop to the basket, while the basket man has the first two perimeter passes."

If the ball was then swung from the top of the key to the wing on either side, the current basket man (X1) would again come out to take the next two perimeter passes, with the current ball man (X2) again dropping quickly to protect the basket (Diagram 1-65).

Diagram 1-65 displays the ball at the point. Should the ball be reversed to the opposite wing, X1 comes out to cover the receiver. X2 drops to protect the basket. X1 now has the next perimeter pass as well as the one he just covered.

The major points of emphasis for the three offensive players (O1, O2, and O3) are:
- The two wing players (O2 and O3) should sprint out and get ahead of the ball, while constantly looking for the pass.
- When the wings hit the free throw line extended, they should plant off their outside feet, and slash cut directly to the basket (while looking to receive a pass).
- O3 should keep the ball in the middle and get down the floor as quickly as possible, but under control.
- O1 should not anticipate that the defense will stop the dribble penetration, and if the defense doesn't stop him, he should then attack the basket until someone does stop him.
- If and when the defense does stop O1, he should make a solid jump stop and look to make a bounce pass (below the outstretched arms of the defenders) to one of the two cutting teammates.
- Offensive players should avoid offensive fouls as a result of out-of-control dribbling or running.
- If the ball is passed into a wing area to a player who is not driving, O1 should follow the pass a few steps to shorten the length of the potential return pass.
- All fast breaking offensive players should remember to take what the defense will give them. The offensive players should not force shots or passes.

The major points of emphasis for the two defensive players (X1 and X2) are:
- Each player should make sure that no question remains as to who has taken the ball man responsibilities and that the other defender has taken the basket man assignment.

- Both players should prevent dribble penetrations and drives to the basket and encourage the offense to pass the ball as often as possible; the more passes the opponents make, the more chance of a turnover and the more time the defense has bought to allow the other defensive teammates to get back to help defend.
- After the ball man has stopped the dribble penetration of the offensive dribbler in the middle and influenced the first pass to the wing, the ball man must immediately drop to the weakside block area, as if he were defending a backdoor cut. That is, he (X1 in Diagram 1-63) would turn his back on the ball and face the weakside block area where 03 will most likely go, looking down his extended right arm for the ball.
- The original basket man (X2 in Diagram 1-63) should take the first and the second perimeter pass by closing out on the ball at a controlled speed.
- Both defenders should remember that once the ball is centered back up (as in Diagram 1-64), the new basket man (X1 in Diagram 1-64) again has the next two passes.

2-on-1 Portion of the Drill (Diagrams 1-66 and 1-67)

When the three offensive players (01, 02, and 03) lose possession of the ball via a made or missed shot, or a turnover, either the shooter or the player who committed

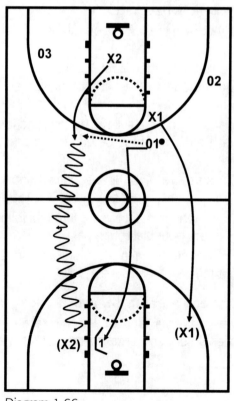

Diagram 1-66

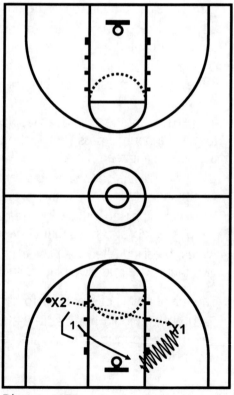

Diagram 1-67

the turnover must turn and sprint back to protect the far basket by himself. The original two defenders (X1 and X2) would then run a two-man offensive fast break against the new lone defender (01 in Diagram 1-66).

The new defender (01) works on his defensive techniques as a solo defender against two offensive opponents (X1 and X2) trying to score an easy basket against his transition defense (Diagram 1-67).

After one shot or turnover, the 2-on-1 action is over. The remaining players then quickly begin to set up the next 3-on-2 scenario, and the drill continues without any interruptions.

The major points of emphasis for the two transitioning offensive players (X1 and X2) are:
- Both players should sprint quickly down the floor under control and looking for defenders as well as the basketball.
- Both should stay widely apart to prevent the one defender from being able to guard both of them.
- Dribblers should not make up their minds what they are going to do ahead of time. Dribblers should have an idea but take what the defense will give to them.
- Offensive players should always remember the phrase "Rebounders jump, while passers stay on the ground." Offensive players should not leave the ground to pass and get lured into an offensive foul, especially when having an offensive numerical advantage.
- Offensive players should look to make bounce passes to teammates who are close to the basket because those types of passes are more difficult for the defender to deflect or intercept.

The major points of emphasis for the lone defensive player (01) are:
- He should get back to protect the basket as quickly as possible.
- He should not worry or sulk about the previously missed shot or the turnover.
- If possible, he should sprint into the lane, and then turn around in the direct path of the dribbler with a wide and sideways stance, somewhat facing the receiver that is without the ball. This stance may seem to be incorrect and a strange stance to be in, but in this manner, the defender has discouraged the dribbler from driving all the way to the basket and is in the best position to be able to defend the cutter who may receive the pass from the dribbler. Being in this specific position/location, the defender has encouraged the dribbler to take a jump shot or to pass the ball to the seemingly open teammate. Being in the sideways stance allows the defender to quickly rotate to the open man, when and if the pass is made. Coaches should use the phrase, "Physically you are here, but mentally you are there" to describe the cat-and-mouse game that the lone defender must play with the two offensive opponents.

- If the pass is then made to the open player (X1), the lone defender (01) should slash at the new offensive driver at an angle so that he would go behind the driver and go for the block. If 01 rushes at the ball handler with his belly facing toward the back of the driver and his right hand going for the ball, it will allow the defender to avoid the light contact and foul. Coaches should not encourage cheap shots or dirty play, but they should tell all defenders that if they are going to foul, to foul in a clean manner so that the offensive opponent cannot get the shot off. The phrase, "No cheap shots, but no kiss fouls!" can be a method of instructing players.
- The lone defender should look to draw an offensive foul before a shot is taken. If the offensive charging foul is not called, a turnover might be caused. A blocking foul could be called, but that isn't as bad as a two-shot shooting foul for the opponents.
- Coaches should constantly remind the lone defender that he is at a numerical disadvantage, and that he is trying to just buy his teammates some time for them to get back to help him. The more passes and dribbling he can influence, the more time it would give his teammates to arrive back to help him defend the basket. Coaches should encourage the defender to be aggressive, but not to go out and attack the dribbler. Use this saying frequently, "Remember that you have something that the bad guys want: the basket. You have something to protect, so stay at home and protect it."

This drill works on specific techniques for the defensive transition as well as the offensive transition. Offensive fundamentals such as passing, catching, dribbling, running, shooting, and quickly getting back on defense are incorporated in this drill on a fast-paced full-court scale. Defensive fundamentals such as stopping dribble penetration, guarding the ball, reacting to passes, defensive box-outs, defensive rebounding, and quick and immediate full-court offensive transition are practiced by the players, and observed by the coaches. For both the offensive and the defensive groups involved in the drill, a certain level of physical conditioning is involved in running full-court sprints.

Summary

Drills are an innovative way to break down offensive and defensive techniques and make sure those techniques are taught by coaches, learned by the players, and practiced so that players can improve on those techniques. Defensively, a coach must be able to teach and coach his players to prevent the opposing teams from getting any easy points. They must instill the philosophy that if an opposing team is going to score, the opponents must have to work and work to earn those points.

Conversely, successful offensive teams know how and are able to score a few easy points in each and every game to counter the tough defenses they will eventually face somewhere in their season.

Drills allow players to be able to run and jump and cut loose with a lot of energy. Drills can be a conditioning drill. Drills are a motivational and inspirational way to start off a practice with all of the movement and structured freedom that can be incorporated into the drill. All drills should combine both offensive and defensive fundamentals and basics into the same fluid and time-efficient drill.

2

Important Pivots of the Ball Handler

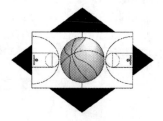

"Unless you plan to outrebound and outshoot everyone you play, then you better learn to handle the ball."
—Coach Henry Iba

An offensive player must first get possession of the basketball before he can become a ball handler. Obtaining possession of the ball may take place in only a few ways. On the defensive end of the floor, the ball handler could get possession of the ball after the opposition has scored by receiving an inbounds pass from a teammate, or after the opposition has missed a shot by getting the defensive rebound or receiving an outlet pass off a defensive rebound. Offensively, the ball could be taken from a sideline out-of-bounds or a baseline out-of-bounds situation, in the frontcourt from an entry or play, or from an actual offensive rebound.

The Inbounds and Outlet Pass Receiver

If the opponent makes his shot, the ball must be taken out-of-bounds and passed inbounds to an offensive player. The offensive pass receiver must first face the out-of-bounds passer to catch the inbounds pass. The pass receiver most often catches the ball while not directly facing his basket. The pass receiver must then catch the ball before turning to face both the basket and the defense that awaits him. For the offensive player who now has the basketball, a pivot must be used to square up and immediately get into triple threat position. What must not ever be forgotten is how important the art of pivoting is to the offensive moves of a ball handler.

In the backcourt, while receiving either inbounds passes or (defensive rebound) outlet passes, the first fundamental is to come back to the ball and meet the pass. While facing the inbounds passer and the ball, the pass receiver (01) loses sight of three vital things. The receiver cannot see any opposing defenders, any offensive teammates that are downcourt, or his actual offensive basket. It is imperative that the ball handler receives the inbounds pass, turns around as quickly and as safely as possible to be able to see these three important things. The safety factor outweighs the quickness factor when receiving an inbounds pass.

The first point that must be made is the establishment of a common language in the actual definitions of the types of pivots that must be utilized. When an offensive player receives the ball while having his back to the basket at both the full-court and the half-court levels, he can pivot away from the basket and potential defenders. This pivot can be defined as a front pivot (even though he is actual stepping away from his offensive basket and potential ball defenders). Another offensive move opposite of this original pivot would be a pivot that has the ball handler pivot toward his basket and defender but could be called a reverse pivot or an inside pivot. Confusion can result here, as calling a pivot that actually places the ball handler immediately closer to the basket is called a reverse pivot. This misconception is caused by the fact that the ball handler has started with his back toward the basket. Another name for this reverse pivot can be accurately called an inside pivot.

The next discussion deals with which foot should be the actual pivot foot: the original outside foot or the inside foot (since his back is initially toward the basket.) Advantages and disadvantages result from both types of pivots by ball handlers who receive the ball while originally starting with their back to the basket. These pluses and minuses will be discussed and presented, with the reader making the evaluation and the ultimate decision on which is more viable and comfortable to that coach's personality and philosophy.

This first discussion is about how a ball handler starts with his back to the basket in a full-court location in the backcourt. Advantages of the so-called front pivot (off the original outside foot) while receiving the inbounds pass with his back to the basket are the following: after the pivot, the ball handler would then have his (new) outside foot as his free foot, and would be able to protect the ball better by keeping the ball away from potential close ball defenders, whether facing one defender or two trapping defenders. The so-called disadvantages of this front pivot could be that this pivot does not allow the ball handler as quick of a view of the basket and his potential pass receivers, since this situation is at the full-court level where the ball handler is not going to be able to catch, pivot and immediately shoot the ball; this assessment somewhat contradicts the footwork that will later be described for offensive players that have their back to the basket and know they will not be immediate shooters off the pass (in frontcourt situations.)

Advantages for ball handlers who receive the inbounds pass in the backcourt and use the so-called reverse pivot or inside pivot (off the original outside foot) could include: this pivot allows the new ball handler possible quicker views of the basket and offensive teammates, and the new outside foot of the ball handler is now the free foot. The disadvantages of this type of pivot include: this quick pivot could result in quick turnovers by the unseen and unsuspected close defenders, and the possible quicker vision of the basket and teammates when in the backcourt is not a true advantage when the chances of a turnover are greater with this pivot.

The pass receivers should first catch the ball and then front pivot off his original outside foot toward the sideline. This pivot is actually a front pivot away from his defender because the receiver initially has his back to the defender. Even though the pivot is turning away from the defender, this pivot is still considered a front pivot because the offensive player is stepping forward from the direction that he is currently facing.

This front pivot turns the ball handler away from the middle where the maximum amount of the defensive pressure most likely would be. This front pivot then allows the new ball handler to first find the defender that is guarding him, then to face the basket and his teammates. From there, the pass receiver can begin to push the ball down the court by passing to another teammate or by dribbling the ball.

While many coaches believe in making the reverse pivot (toward the defense) after the catch because they can quickly see the court and their teammates downcourt, it is safer to use the front pivot (away from the defense) to prevent any surprise defensive pressure that is not anticipated. Also, the safety of the basketball is worth the very minute time lost in sighting a teammate downcourt by using the front pivot instead of the reverse pivot. Diagram 2-1 shows an example of an offensive player (O1) receiving

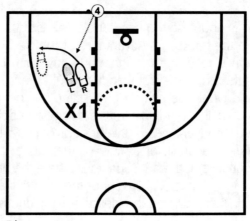

Diagram 2-1

an inbounds pass in the backcourt (from 04) and front pivoting off the outside foot (in this case, it is the left foot).

Diagram 2-2 illustrates the same inbounds situation, but with the ball handler (03) on the opposite side of the court. That ball handler, as well, meets the pass (from 04) and then also front pivots off his outside foot and then looks to advance the ball via pass or dribble. In this case, the outside foot is the right foot and the free foot is the left foot on this particular side of the court.

Diagram 2-3 shows an example of an offensive player (02) receiving an outlet pass (after a defensive rebound by 05) with the pass receiver on the transition offense's left side of the backcourt. The pass receiver is facing the rebounder and has his back to his own offensive basket at the other end of the court. He cannot see any offensive teammates, his basket, or any defender near him. The pass receiver should meet the pass, front pivot off the outside foot (on this side of the floor it is the right foot), and search for defenders, offensive teammates, and the basket downcourt, before advancing the ball downcourt.

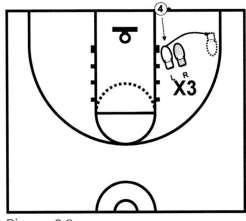

Diagram 2-2

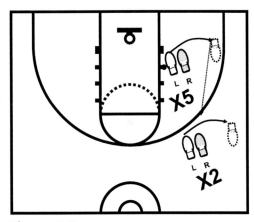

Diagram 2-3

The potential pass receiver (02) is not the only offensive player involved with the all-important pivot. In order to obtain the defensive rebound, that player (05) has had to also carry out two pivots. The first was in his execution of a defensive box-out on his opponent, which will be discussed more thoroughly in Chapter 7. The second pivot is when the defensive rebounder turns to locate a pass receiver and then make the outlet pass to trigger the fast break. This action is also illustrated in Diagram 2-3 and it shows an example of the defensive rebounder (05) getting the rebound on a particular side of the court, while facing the opponent's basket and therefore having his back toward his own offensive basket and facing away from the opposition's pressure. On this particular side of the court, this makes the right foot of the defensive rebounder the outside foot and therefore the pivot foot. The defensive rebounder with the basketball should make a front pivot off the outside foot (right) to sight the teammate (02), before making the outlet pass. As shown, both the defensive rebounder/outlet passer and the outlet pass receiver who receives that pass both make front pivots (away from pressure) off the outside foot before then facing their own basket.

When the ball is advanced by passing the ball down the floor, a pass receiver in the frontcourt could very well likely also have his back to his own basket. He must catch the ball, face the basket quickly, carefully, and immediately become a threat to the defense. This ending position is traditionally called the triple-threat position, being a threat to the defense via passing, driving, and/or shooting the basketball.

Taking Possession From the Turnover or the Actual Defensive Rebound

When the original defender has his back to his own basket, the footwork of acquiring possession of the ball after an opponent's turnover or the actual defensive rebound would simply be the same as receiving an inbounds or outlet pass. If the defender is facing his own basket when he secures possession of the ball, then the footwork is simply to advance the ball downcourt.

Frontcourt Pass Receiving

A pass receiver might have to pop out after a V-cut or off a down screen, or use other means to get open, whether the situation is an inbounded ball or a frontcourt entry/play scenario. Versus the backcourt full-court situation, a pass receiver in the frontcourt is more of an immediate threat to the defense, especially after the ball is passed to him. With the back originally to the basket, a reverse pivot (that is actually towards the basket) off the original outside foot (right foot) would swing the free foot (left foot) farther to the outside, placing the ball handler farther to the outside or towards the baseline. If the cutter (O3) is sure that he is not going to shoot the basketball immediately off this pass, he should reverse pivot off the outside (right) foot, which allows him to have his (new) outside foot (closest to the baseline) as the free foot after catching the pass (Diagram 2-4).

An offensive player receiving the pass with his back to the basket (O3 in Diagram 2-4) who makes a front pivot (that is actually away from the offensive basket) off the original inside foot (left, in this case) will be able to get to the basket more quickly, because he will be closer to the basket and to the middle of the court. More importantly, he will be able to get the shot off more quickly. Therefore, if the cutter is expecting to shoot immediately off this pass, O3 should make a front pivot off his inside (left) heel so that he can catch the pass and quickly go up to take his shot.

Coaches should stress for the cutter/shooter these important techniques: get the hands into shooting position, give the passer a target, and pivot off the inside heel.

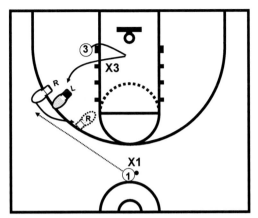

Diagram 2-4

All pivots must be made at the exact moment the receiver catches the ball to avoid a traveling call. When the inside foot is the pivot foot, the heel of that foot should be driven hard to the floor for two important reasons. The heel pivot stops the momentum of the cutter (or dribbler), and keeps the shooter from floating or drifting after taking the shot off the pass (or the dribble.). This pivot allows the shooter to jump straight up vertically and come back down in a somewhat straight line. Coaches never want a jump shooter to fall away or to drift. Using the inside heel pivot helps diminish the momentum that causes these two fatal flaws in a player's jump shot.

The heel, besides acting as a brake for the cutter, also allows for a very smooth and fluid front pivot. Pivoting off of the inside heel is a smooth and fluid pivot that will speed up the time of the pivot, getting the shooter squared up to the basket in a much quicker fashion. These two techniques will give the receiver/shooter much more of an opportunity to get the shot off quicker and therefore increase the chance of an effective and accurate shot.

Pivoting off the inside heel is a smooth and fluid pivot that will speed up the time of the pivot, getting the shooter squared up to the basket in a much quicker fashion. These two techniques will give the receiver/shooter much more of an opportunity to get the shot off quicker and therefore increase the chance of an effective and accurate shot.

Initially, the offensive pass receiver has his back toward the same three important items as when in the backcourt: the opposition's defense, offensive teammates, and the offensive team's own goal. Coaches should want the offensive pass receiver to catch the ball, immediately front pivot away from the defender who is immediately behind him, and get in position to become an immediate threat to the opposition's defense.

Being in the frontcourt with the back to the basket, coaches should want those offensive players who are expecting to immediately shoot off the pass to front pivot off the inside heel. After making this pivot and facing the basket, the free foot is now the inside foot. This pivot places the offensive ball handler facing and much closer to the basket, making the ball handler more of a serious shooting and/or driving threat.

Diagram 2-4 shows the pass receiver (03) popping out to the wing on the offense's left side. With the offensive cutter's back to the basket, his initial inside foot is the left foot and the free foot is the right foot. The cutter should front pivot off that left foot (his heel) away from the defender who is behind him to immediately face the basket and be in position to quickly shoot off the pass.

Diagram 2-5 shows a pass receiver (02) receiving a down screen (from 04) on the right side of the offense's frontcourt. With his back to the offensive basket, 02's first inside foot is the right foot (and the outside foot is the left foot). Therefore, the pass receiver (02) that is wanting and expecting to shoot quickly off the pass has to front pivot off the right foot (heel) at the same instant he is catching the pass. This technique will allow the pass receiver to be able to immediately square up to the basket in the proper triple threat offensive position so he can shoot, drive, or pass.

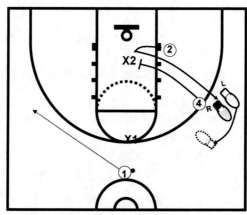

Diagram 2-5

Pass Receivers Who Are Not Instant Shooters

Many coaches want frontcourt offensive players who receive the ball and are facing the basket on the perimeter but are not instant shooters off the pass to have the outside foot (when facing the basket) to be the designated free foot. This approach is the opposite of those offensive players who break out originally with the back to the basket before receiving the pass and squaring up to the basket to become immediate shooters off that pass. The previously discussed contradiction (in the backcourt scenarios) can only be settled by coaching staffs willing to teach their offensive players a second technique.

This second technique obviously will require more teaching effort by coaches and more learning effort by players, but the mixture of these two techniques can be very successful. Coaches simply must tell their offensive players, who start with their back to the basket as they catch the ball and are wanting to quickly shoot off the pass, to pivot off the inside foot (heel). Coaches would then tell those same players that when they are popping out to catch the ball and expecting not to instantly shoot off the pass that they are to make a reverse pivot (toward the basket and toward the defender) with the original outside foot.

This contradiction of the footwork techniques gives the new ball handler his inside foot as his pivot foot when facing the basket and his baseline (or outside) foot as his free foot. This approach is better for offensive players who are not expecting to immediately shoot, but who are more of a passing threat to the opposition.

Diagram 2-6 shows an offensive player (O3) popping out to the free throw line extended on the offense's left side of the court. With his back to the basket, O3's initial inside foot is the left foot. If O3 is reasonably confident of not catching and immediately shooting off the pass, then O3 should make a (reverse or inside) pivot immediately toward the defender and toward his basket off the right (or the original outside) foot.

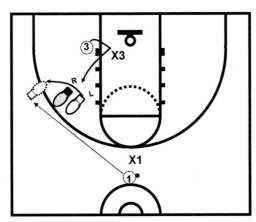

Diagram 2-6

After catching and simultaneously making this reverse pivot, the ball handler is facing the basket in triple-threat position with his new outside foot (left) as his free foot. Naturally, his right foot is the pivot foot and is on the inside.

These two techniques can be taught to offensive players and still kept relatively simple. The key in the decision is whether the pass receivers think they will be instant shooters off the pass or not.

Pass Receivers Who Are Instant Shooters

If the ball handler is already facing the basket before he catches the pass, his inside foot is opposite the inside foot when he starts with his back is toward the basket. A player who is already facing the basket would be in that particular position as a dribbler or after receiving a pass off some flare screens, certain back screens, most ball screens, or he is originally lined up facing the basket in the particular offensive set the team is utilizing.

Diagram 2-7 shows the example of a dribbler (O1) passing the ball (to O2) before making a flare cut off O3's flare screen (on the offense's left side of the court) and receiving the pass (from O2) while already facing the basket. O1's inside foot remains the right foot (with the left foot being the outside foot and also the free foot). He should pivot off the inside (right) heel as he catches the basketball. O1 is now in triple-threat position, ready to instantly shoot, drive, or pass the basketball.

Diagram 2-8 shows an offensive cutter (O2) receiving a back screen near the elbow area (set by O5) while shuffle cutting toward the ball and the basket from the right side of the court. In this particular situation, the cutter's inside foot is the right foot. In this case, this offensive cutter is already halfway facing the basket. The cutter/pass receiver (O2) should pivot off the right (inside) heel at the exact moment that O3's pass hits his hands so that he can immediately square up to the basket, becoming an instant shooting, driving, and passing threat to the defense.

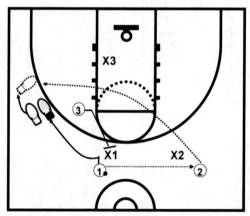
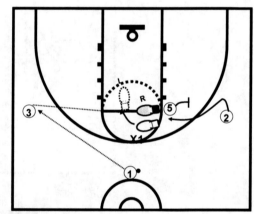

Diagram 2-7

Diagram 2-8

Dribblers and Screeners

Diagram 2-9 gives an illustration of the traditional ball screen and O1 dribble scraping off O5's ball screen toward the offense's right side of the court. O1 comes off O5's ball screen while facing the basket and pulls up for a jump shot. The technique would have him front pivoting off the left heel (still the inside foot) and by swinging his free foot (right) around to square up to the basket, allowing him to either get the shot off quickly or to pass the ball to a teammate.

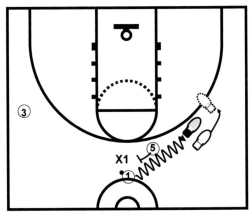

Diagram 2-9

If the dribbler were to dribble scrape off a ball screen on the left side of the court, the dribbler's inside foot would be the right foot, and his outside (left) foot would be the free foot. When he pulled up to take the jump shot, he would have to front pivot off his right (inside) heel and swing his left (outside in this case) foot around to square up for the shot or the pass.

The ball screener (05) can make many offensive moves after his ball screen is used by the dribbler (01). Some of these moves include: the screen roll, slipping the screen, going to set an off-the-ball screen on a second teammate, or receiving a screen from a teammate to implement the screen-the-screener offensive action. Only the screen roll offensive action will be discussed.

Diagram 2-10 illustrates 05 setting a ball screen for 01 to use to his advantage. As soon as 01 makes contact with 05's outside shoulder (left shoulder, in this case), the

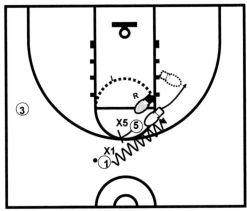

Diagram 2-10

screener (05) should reverse pivot off his inside foot (right foot, in this example) while swinging his free (left) foot toward the basket. This technique allows 05 to constantly face both 01 and the basketball as he rolls to the basket and as 01 dribbles toward the basket.

Once the ball handler is facing his own offensive basket, one of his offensive threats is the dribble. An offensive player has three main reasons to dribble:
- To advance the ball toward the offensive basket
- To improve passing angles (to teammates)
- To get out of trouble with the defense

When the dribbler is in the frontcourt not completely facing the basket and he kills the dribble, the dribbler should front pivot off the inside foot to fully square up to the basket. If the dribbler does not become a shooter, he is still a potential passer.

Coaching staffs should have a series of offensive moves and counter moves that are designed to attack or counteract the opposition's defense. Coaching staffs should thoroughly teach, practice, and drill these techniques daily in practice until every player can successfully execute the offensive moves. Coaches must expect all ball handlers to execute these moves each time they are offensive passers both in the backcourt and in the frontcourt.

While in the frontcourt, a jump stop can be made and the inside foot should be the new pivot foot, while the outside foot should be the free foot—the foot that can move and step outside of the defender's feet so that the dribbler/passer is able to make a pass to a teammate. If the pass receiver does not take the shot, the passer should protect the ball by placing the ball on the outside of the knee of the outside (free) leg.

1-on-1 Pivoting Techniques

The two-foot jump stop, described in Chapter 1, is the first phase in this ballhandling and ball protection technique. The second phase is the step-out. In the descriptively named step-out phase, coaches should have the passer step horizontally to the outside or to the right (if the right foot is the outside foot) to see if he can outflank the defense, while still protecting the ball beside the passer's free knee. The phrases used to help describe this step of the series of moves are *protect the ball* and *step outside of the defense*. If the passer should pass the ball, that pass is determined by the phrase: "If your foot is outside of the defense's foot, look to pass over or under the defender." This phrase simply means that the ball handler should first attack the defender's outside foot, and if that is successful and the team is able to pass the ball, he should then pass either over or under the defender's outstretched arm and hand. The teaching phrases used in this situation are: fake high and go low, or fake low and go high. Another point of emphasis is for the passer to step out wide, but not so wide that he becomes too extended and off balance.

Diagram 2-11 is an illustration of the step-out phase, which features a passer on the right side of the frontcourt, making the inside foot the left foot and the pivot foot, and the outside foot the right foot, otherwise called the free foot. The passer steps horizontally to the right (with the right foot) and looks to pass the ball if his (right) foot beats the defense's (left) foot. Another teaching phrase that should be used to make sure that the passer steps in a 100 percent lateral direction is: "Step due east or due west—not north or south." This command is a way of telling the offensive passer not to step either away from the defender or toward the defender, but to attempt to step laterally around the defender and his feet.

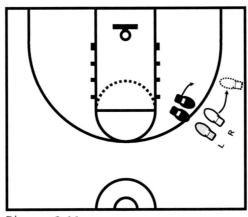

Diagram 2-11

If the defender steps in the same direction (horizontally to his left) as the passer steps (horizontally to his right), the passer faces increasingly more difficulty to make the pass. If the ball handler's foot is not outside of the defender's foot, an offensive counter move must be executed. This offensive counter move to the defense's reaction is the third phase of the offensive technique.

This phase is called the rip-through move. With the ball still firmly protected beside the outside knee, the passer should rip the ball low and hard across the shoe tops as both the ball and the outside free leg complete a front pivot in front of the defender. The ball is held strongly with both hands just inches above the floor (away from the defender's hands) until the free foot lands laterally outside of the defender's foot that is opposite of the original foot. As the ball is being quickly and strongly pulled across, the free leg immediately follows in the same motion to help protect the basketball. The ball is then placed beside the (same free) knee, again protecting the ball from the defender.

Most defenders will not get that low with their hands, when the ball is ripped across the shoe tops in front of the defender. Most defenders are unable to steal the ball when it is pulled across quickly and low just inches from the floor.

Key points of emphasis of this third phase are that the passer should step due west and attempt to step outside the defender's leg (with the ball still protected beside the free knee). The step should not be too much of an extended step. The passer should remain balanced and not overextended. If the passer's free foot beats the defender's foot, the passer should be able to pass the ball over or under the defender's arm and hand and the pass is successfully executed.

The ball handler now has his back somewhat toward the defender and the pass receiver. The passer should still have the ball protected beside the knee of the free leg and can make the pass with the same hand. The same hand is used, but that hand is on the other side of the ball and in a somewhat cupped position. Since the ball handler is somewhat turned away from his defender, another coaching point of emphasis is to stress that the ball handler/passer must look to make sure that the receiver is open before making the actual pass.

Diagram 2-12 illustrates the third phase of the technique when the passer makes the first front pivot across the face of the defender. In this situation, the third phase is from the right side of the court with the inside foot or left foot as the pivot foot. The free foot is the right foot, and the passer has attempted to step outside of the defender's right foot with his free foot.

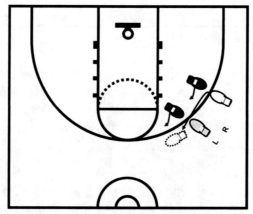

Diagram 2-12

After the initial front pivot, if the defender reacts to the ball handler's moves and techniques, the defender could again step laterally in the same direction of the ball handler and discourage or prevent the pass from being made. If so, the fourth and final phase can begin.

The descriptively named swing-around phase is the last of the series of offensive moves that the ball handler could make. The offensive ball handler's counter move to this second reaction of the defender is to then make a second front pivot (in one complete step) and swing around back to the initial side of his attack. Even though this move is still a front pivot, this pivot is actually made away from the defender and the basket because the passer has his back turned to the defender. The same points of emphasis of the pivot and the pass are emphasized by the coaching staff:

- "Do not extend the step-out too far, but try to step outside the defender's foot."
- "Protect the ball beside the knee of the free leg."
- "Step due east."
- "Fake high to go low" or "Fake low to go high."

Diagram 2-13 shows the fourth phase of the ball handler. It has the defender not allowing himself to be outflanked by the ball handler on the offense's left side, and therefore forcing the ball handler to make the second front pivot.

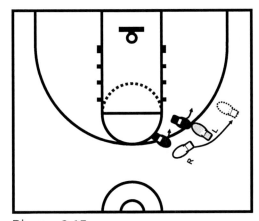

Diagram 2-13

Remember, this pivot is actually considered a front pivot, but this pivot actually turns away from the defensive pressure because the offensive passer now has his back toward the defense. If the ball handler is successful with this final phase of the technique, the passer's right foot (free) is laterally outside of the defender's left foot, which allows the passer to make an unguarded pass to a teammate. If the passer's foot beats the defender's foot, the passer can again fake low to go high (or fake high to go low) and make the pass.

If the defense again reacts to the offensive movement, the passer could repeat the phases of the pivoting techniques or pass the ball to a teammate who is more of a safety valve receiver. This new receiver would have less defensive pressure applied to him.

Obviously, the same techniques will work with all passers located on the left side of the floor. With the passer facing the basket and being on the left side of the court, the outside foot is now the left foot, with the inside foot still the pivot foot. The first move (the step-out move) should be for the passer to step with the outside (left) foot laterally to his left (step due west) and to keep the ball safely protected beside the knee of the left (the free or the outside) leg.

If the step-out move is unsuccessful, the rip-through move (the first front pivot off the right pivot foot) should be made with the left leg stepping across low and hard across the shoe tops in front of the defense. As the ball is pulled across near the floor, the free leg quickly follows behind the ball and continues to attempt to step outside the defender's left foot. If the passer's free foot is outside of the defender's foot, the chance of a successful pass is much greater.

If the step-out and the rip-through moves are successfully defended by the defense, the swing-through move must be used. If the free foot of the passer is not laterally outside of the defender's foot, the passer (whose back is now turned away from the defender) should make the second front pivot (this time away from the defense). The passer is trying to outflank the defender by attempting to place his free foot outside of the defender's foot. If the passer's foot is outside of the defender's foot, the passer should again fake high and go low or fake low and go high to make the pass. If the pivot attempt is unsuccessful, the passer may have to look to make a pass that is not as close to the basket as the initial pass receiver.

Dribbling and Driving Techniques

Dribbling and driving is an essential part of any offensive attack, whether it is a man or zone offense. The dribbling penetration can provide very close shots for the driver or for teammates either inside or on the perimeter. If the original defender cannot effectively stop the penetration, an additional defender or two must help. Drawing more than one defender on the ball obviously causes the opposition's defense to try to defend the four off-the-ball offensive players with only three defensive players.

In the last couple of seasons, one of the newest man offensive raves, ironically, is called the dribble drive offense. This newest offensive attack should only reinforce the importance of proper footwork by offensive ball handlers.

When the dribbler penetrates the defense with an attacking dribble, and then passes to a teammate on the inside, the offensive play is called the drive and dump. When the ball is driven and then passed out to an offensive teammate on the perimeter, this offensive action is called the penetrate and pitch. Both types of play are simple to utilize if and only if the driver can make an attacking drive to the basket. Hence, it is very important that all dribblers are able to execute the proper techniques to successfully drive on the opposition's on-the-ball defense.

If the pass receiver starts with his back to the basket before breaking open on the perimeter, and if he has made the decision that he will not shoot off the pass, the receiver will use the original outside foot as the pivot foot as he makes the catch. He then would have to make a reverse pivot or an inside pivot (actually toward his defender) off his left foot on the offense's right side of the court. Since the ball handler has decided to become a driver/dribbler, the ball handler first would obviously have to keep the new inside foot (left) as the pivot foot.

If the shot is not obtainable and making a pass is not available, the ball handler should then look to drive or to attack the defense with a dribble. Often, the ball handler can free himself for the drive/dribble after making a shot fake. The shot fake must be a realistic shot fake—that is, the shot fake must look like his actual shot. One of the best techniques in shot faking (before driving) is to make the shot fake not too quick, but slow enough for the defender to react to the shot fake. Another good technique is to bring the ball up through the face and look at the rim.

When the defender reacts to the realistic fake, the offensive ball handler must immediately start the proper dribbling techniques. The driver should first place the ball in a protected area, where the ball cannot be stolen, slapped away, or deflected. The ideal location for a driver who has not killed his dribble is to place the ball beside the knee of the free leg. This location has the knee between the defender and the ball and therefore protects the ball from the defender.

If the driver wants to then attack the ball defender, he can look to attack the lead foot of the defender. If the lead foot of the defender is on the same side as the free foot of the ball handler, the ball handler should make a simple blast move. This move is basically the dribbler driving in more of a straight-ahead direction against the ball defender. It should be remembered that passers only should step east or west—not north or south; while drivers should step north—not east or west.

When driving, the dribbler should step with the free foot in the direction of the shoulder of the defender's lead foot. The teaching and coaching phrases used to describe this technique are: "Attack the lead foot of the defender" and "Scrape off the defender's shoulder to cut off the defender's angle of pursuit."

The third coaching phrase in this dribbling/driving situation is to tell the dribbler to step north. Stepping almost directly toward the defender allows no room or space for the defender to react and attempt to cut off the path of the dribbler. Scraping off the defender's shoulder is very important because it prevents the defender from having any angle of pursuit on the driver once the dribbler is around or past the defender. If the driver steps laterally and away from the defender, it provides the defender the needed space to recover and possibly cut off the dribbler on his drive. Stepping more toward the defender makes the dribbler more aggressive and puts the defender at a great disadvantage, making it difficult for the defender to recover.

A misconception of many dribblers is to try to avoid the defender by laterally going around the defender. If the same concept was applied to passers and the initial step-out was defended, stepping forward in this manner would not allow the passer to then front pivot and try to attack the opposite side of the defender.

The direction of the first step of the passer is different than that of the first step of the dribbler. Diagram 2-14 shows an example of the dribbler being on the right side of the court with the defender having his outside foot (left) up as the lead foot.

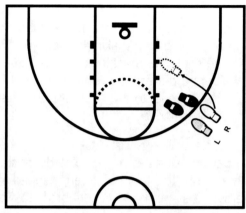

Diagram 2-14

The dribbler should have his inside foot (left) as the pivot foot, so the dribbler's free foot (right) is the attacking foot. The dribbler's right foot then would attack the defender's left foot by stepping almost directly at the defender. The dribbler would scrape off the defender by stepping with the outside foot (right) past the defender's left side. The ball should be placed beside the knee of the free leg (right), and as that foot completes the first step, the ball should be placed ahead to make the first dribble. From there, the dribbler can continue the dribbling attack on the defender with more dribbles, if necessary.

If the inside foot of the defender (the right foot) is the lead foot, the dribbler should attack that lead foot. If the outside foot of the dribbler (the right foot) is the free foot, the dribbler must make what is called a front crossover move. This move is done with the dribbler protecting the ball beside the knee of the free leg (outside leg—the right leg, in this case). As the ball is ripped low and hard across the shoe tops, the free leg and foot follow the path of the ball, step north, and scrape off the defender's right shoulder.

The first step should be made near the defender (to cut off the defender's angle of pursuit) with the ball still protected beside the knee. As the foot of the free leg touches the floor, the ball handler initiates the first dribble with the hand that is away from the defense (the left hand, in this instance).

Diagram 2-15 illustrates the dribbler making a front crossover move that includes a front pivot toward the defender's shoulder, immediately followed by a dribble. The driver's free foot (right foot) steps across and scrapes off the right shoulder of the defender before making the dribble with the left hand. A good defender would make a swing step (front pivot) to try to regain the advantage (see Chapter 7 for defensive footwork).

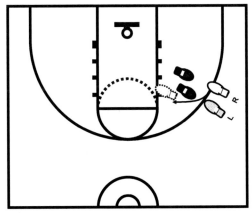

Diagram 2-15

Pivoting While Being Trapped

If the ball handler is caught in a double-team trap by the defense, the three phases of the offensive techniques of passing out of a trap have to be moderately adjusted. Using the free foot to step out, coaches should teach the ball handler to initially attack the trapping defender's outside foot that is on the side of his free foot, and use the step-out move.

Diagram 2-16 illustrates a ball handler being trapped by two defenders (X1 on the ball handler's left side, and X2 being the defender on the ball handler's right side) with the ball handler's free foot being the right foot. The step-out move is shown with the ball handler stepping directly to his right with his right foot, while protecting the ball beside the right knee. If his right foot can step outside of the X2's left foot, he should

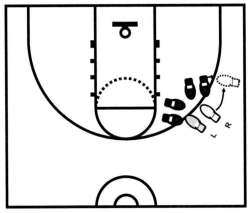

Diagram 2-16

be able to pass over or under the outstretched left hand of X2. The same coaching phrases should be used:

- "Step east or west—not north or south."
- "Protect the ball beside the knee."
- "If your foot beats his foot, look to pass."
- "Fake high and go low" or "Fake low and go high" to make the pass.

If the defender steps out so that the passer's foot doesn't beat the defender's foot, then the ball handler front pivots and rips the ball low and hard across the shoe tops to attack the outside foot of the second defender. This same rip-through move is used against one defender, but now the other defender's outside shoulder and foot are attacked.

Diagram 2-17 illustrates the same ball handler being trapped by the same two defenders. In this diagram, the step-out move is defended, and the ball handler immediately goes to the rip-through move to attack the outside of the second trapping defender. The ball handler makes a front pivot and rips the ball through and across the shoe tops. Most defenders will not get their hands low enough to steal the ball that is being swung quickly and mere inches off the floor. If the ball handler's (outside) free foot is outside X1's right foot, the pass can be made. The passer may have to fake low to go high or fake high to go low. The player uses the same techniques in attacking the trap as he does in attacking one defender.

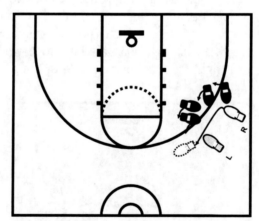

Diagram 2-17

A slightly different technique is used if the second defender also laterally steps out to discourage the ball handler from making the pass. The ball handler makes the swing-around move, the second front pivot away from the defense. If the two defensive trappers have both successfully defended the offense's attempts to attack the defense by outflanking them, maybe both defenders have spread themselves too thin.

Diagram 2-18 illustrates the ball handler being trapped and unable to make the pass on the outside of either defender. The ball handler should then make the swing around move, just as he does against one defender—with one exception. If X2 protected his outside and X1 protected his outside, the ball handler now probes the area between the two trappers.

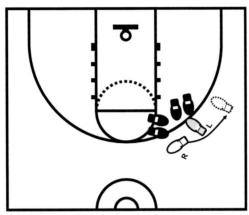

Diagram 2-18

On the swing around move, the second front pivot that is now away from the defense should be made in the same manner as before. The only exception is that the step with the right foot goes only as far as the space between the two trappers. The ball handler then steps through both defenders.

The ball is squeezed with both hands to protect the ball from both defenders, with both elbows extending out. This technique further protects the ball from the reaching and slapping hands of the defenders. The lowered head also protects the ball. This move can be described as a fullback taking the handoff and going into the defensive line.

The eyes must be up to see and to not bowl over the trappers, committing an offensive foul. The ball handler does not overextend himself and become off balanced, committing a traveling violation. Once he has split the trap, the ball handler looks to pass the ball out of the trap. With two defenders on the ball handler, the offense now has four off-the-ball pass receivers who must be defended by only three defensive opponents. Somebody must be open. When that pass is successfully completed, the offense has a fast break advantage over the opposition and should capitalize on that advantage.

The swing-around move does not come back to the original flank of the defense. Instead, the swing around step goes only back halfway. The swing around step attacks the weakened middle of the trappers, by going in between the two defenders.

After the second front pivot is made, the ball handler looks to split the trap and step through the trap with the ball handler's body protecting the ball. The ball handler pulls the ball in close to the upper chest, and as the step is made between the trappers with the free foot, the ball handler slightly lowers his head and chins the ball. The elbows are placed out, protecting the ball from the defenders. The ball handler remains balanced and under control. Once the ball handler has stepped through the trap, the head comes up to search for an open teammate to whom he can pass the ball.

Pivot-and-Pass Drill

The pivot-and-pass drill is part of the fundamentals and stretching routine discussed in Chapter 1. In the drill, three players are placed in each group. Each player works on specific offensive (and some defensive) fundamentals. One player works on pivoting and then passing the ball to an offensive teammate, who works on pivoting as the catch is made. After he makes the simultaneous pivot and catch, he immediately shoots the ball (with the proper shooting form) back to the original passer. The third player in the drill plays defense only on the passer.

Diagram 2-19 illustrates a second setup of the pivot-and-pass drill, with 01 being the first passer, X2 being the first defender, and 03 being the first pass receiver/shooter. After 55 seconds, 01 becomes the next defender, X2 becomes the next receiver/shooter, and 03 rotates to become the next passer. The rotation takes place again 55 seconds later, with all three players rotating stations. In three minutes, the entire squad will have played all three fundamental stations. Going hard for 55 seconds and then using five seconds for the transition from one position to the next tends to increase the intensity level.

A small area can include four groups of players performing this drill, which makes up an entire 12-man team. One coach can easily observe this area.

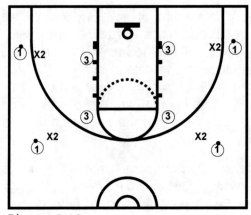

Diagram 2-19

During practice, the pivot-and-pass drill can be executed following any killed dribble by the ball handler. The coach merely needs a signal, like two quick whistles, to activate the drill.

Diagram 2-20 exhibits the pivot-and-pass techniques being used in two ways: first against solo defenders and then against trapping double-teaming defenders. First, have the entire squad perform the drill at the same time, in the same general area of the court. This method allows one (or more) coaches to more easily observe, evaluate, teach, critique, and correct every player that is performing the drill.

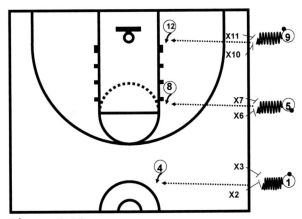

Diagram 2-20

Secondly, have the passers start the drill by dribbling toward the defender. The location is somewhat different, in that the dribblers actually start out-of-bounds on one of the sidelines. Coaches should always have the dribbler/passer dribble to the defense, who must be positioned on the actual sideline. The dribbler should kill his dribble and take a small bunny hop to land simultaneously on both feet. This move allows the ball handler to still have the freedom to choose which foot is the free foot and which foot is the pivot foot.

Always have the dribbler kill his dribble on the actual sideline. In this way, both the players and the coaching staff can use the sideline as a visual reference to see if the passers are truly stepping due east or west. During any of the phases, the coaching staff can easily monitor if the steps are where they are supposed to be. Players can also more easily scrutinize and correct themselves. Sometimes, coaches should place the same 55-second (or longer) time limit for the players.

Coaches can increase the intensity level with winners and losers between the passers and the defenders and they keep score. Successful passes could be worth +1, traveling or bad passes are worth -2, and deflected passes are worth -1. If the offensive players have a positive score, they win. If the offensive players in the drill have a negative score, the defensive team wins. The winning players get to shoot free throws, while the losing players must run some form of sprints while dribbling the basketball for one minute or so.

On the second sequence of three minutes, the passers and shooters work on using the opposite foot as the pivot foot. Thus, in a matter of just six minutes, each player involved in the pivot-and-pass drill have had almost two minutes of pivoting and passing the basketball (using both feet as the pivot foot), two minutes of playing some on-the-ball defense, and two minutes of cutting, catching, and shooting the basketball (using both feet as the pivot foot).

This drill is an intense, productive, and very time efficient drill. Ballhandling is such an important part of the offensive game that all of the necessary fundamentals in regards to successful ballhandling must be thoroughly taught by the coaching staff, completely learned by the players, and drilled and practiced continually by the players and coaches. This drill covers a multitude of those fundamentals in one quick, intense, and useful drill, in a manner that makes it easy for the coaching staff to evaluate and correct each and every participant involved in the drill.

The second way the drill should be used is to prepare offensive ball handlers to attack trapping defenders. The same format is used with the exception that four players must be involved in the drill. So instead of having four groups of three players, coaches can use three groups of four players. Also, the drill to practice offensive skills in attacking trapping defenses will take four minutes in repetition (instead of three minutes). The third slight difference is to place the pass receiver/shooter farther from the dribbler/ passer and emphasize to the pass receiver to break up aggressively and meet every pass.

Coaches place the two trappers (instead of the one defender) on the same sideline with the offensive players in the same locations. The rotation would be 01 (the original dribbler/passer) moves to X2's spot (the trapper on the left), while X2 moves to X3's spot (the original trapper on the right), while X3 rotates to 04's spot (the original pass receiver/shooter), and 04 becomes the next dribbler/passer. After just four minutes, all four players have rotated to the four positions.

Another four minutes can be used so that each player can practice his skills using the opposite foot as the pivot foot (when they are the dribbler/passer and when they are the pass receiver/shooter). With all the offensive (as well as defensive) fundamentals practiced, you will have used only eight minutes of practiced.

Mass Ballhandling and Pivoting Drill

Diagram 2-21 illustrates another mass drill featuring ball handlers against trapping defenders. In this drill, the initial passer (01 in the diagram) uses the same techniques of pivoting and passing to defeat the initial trapping defense (of X2 and X3).

The first pass receiver (04 in Diagram 2-21 and 010 in Diagram 2-22) works on the various important offensive fundamentals such as:

- Meeting the pass
- Protecting the catch with his body (by turning his body slightly before and as the catch is made)
- Pivoting away from the defense (or manager)
- Extending the pass to a second cutting teammate (05 or 011)
- Having the second receiver cut, catch the ball, and then shoot the ball with a power shot (05 in Diagram 2-21 and 011 in Diagram 2-22)

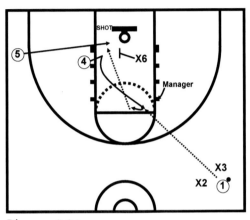

Diagram 2-21

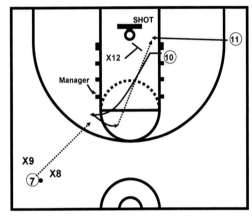

Diagram 2-22

The first pass receiver/second passer (04 in Diagram 2-21 and 010 in Diagram 2-22) must work on the proper offensive fundamentals of pivoting. This drill emphasizes the offensive concept: "Whenever the ball is passed into the middle of a trapping defense, look to immediately extend the pass to another teammate."

Diagrams 2-21 and 2-22 show the general setup of the drill. Diagram 2-21 shows the setup with the offense initially attacking from the right side of the court, while Diagram 2-22 shows the offense beginning its attack of half-court pressure from the left side of the floor. The administration of this drill could be left up to the coaching staff's discretion, but it is suggested that all five players stay in the same positions for three or four repetitions, before rotating (01 to X2 to X3 to 04 to 05). Keeping the players in the specific positions they play in during the games is another way to run the drill.

Summary

Without ballhandling skills, an offensive team fails. The offense can never make use of their other skills. For example, an offensive team has great post players who can score efficiently from the inside. Those post players cannot excel at what they do best if that team cannot deliver the ball to those specific players. Assuming that a team has a very good half-court offense filled with great perimeter shooters, if that team cannot advance the ball into the frontcourt, then those offensive shooting skills and talents are wasted.

Without the basic fundamentals of passing the basketball to advance the ball into the frontcourt or to get the ball into the hands of the dominant scorers within the offense, the offense will be ineffective and wasted.

Without the basic fundamentals of dribbling, an offense will struggle with advancing the ball toward its basket. As important as passing, catching, and dribbling are to the offensive schemes a team possesses, it is still the most elementary fundamental skill. Pivoting actually precedes the two skills of passing and dribbling. Pivoting is the most elementary skill needed to perform the fundamental skills of catching, passing, and dribbling the basketball. The ultimate importance of the skill of pivoting and the proper techniques of pivoting must be addressed by both coaching staffs and players.

As important as ballhandling is to the overall offensive schemes, the art of pivoting is more important. Thus, the art of pivoting is essential to the offensive success of a basketball team. Players who cannot pivot cannot get into proper position to dribble or pass without committing a turnover.

3

Important Pivots of the Shooter

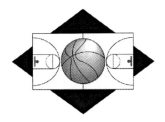

"Shooting makes up for a multitude of sins."
—Coach Hubie Brown

An old adage in basketball goes as follows: "Offense wins games, but defense wins championships." That statement is very accurate, particularly for defense-minded basketball coaches. But despite that firm belief, it is widely known that the greatest defense your team can play will not hold your opponent scoreless. So in order to win, a team must be able to score. To be able to score, a team must be able to shoot the basketball well. How many times have you seen a team run a great offense with good crisp passing, cutting, screening, and intelligent movement of all five offensive players that produces good shot opportunities and not score because of poor shooting?

Good offensive teams must have good shooters and an offensive scheme that can free up those shooters. Shooters' shoulders must be completely squared up to the basket in locations on the court where the shooter can score. Offensive schemes must provide the shots where the least amount of defensive resistance exists.

All shooters shoot the basketball better with the least amount of defensive pressure on them. A team's offensive schemes can help eliminate that defensive pressure, but each individual offensive player must help reduce the amount of defensive pressure placed upon his shot. Offensive shooters use time-proven techniques and methods prior to the actual taking of the shot to produce their own space and distance from their defenders and therefore reduce the pressure on them. Again, the art of pivoting is essential to the offensive moves of a shooter.

Shooters must always be in the process of getting their feet and hands ready even before they receive a pass. *Getting the feet and hands ready* is a phrase that simply means that the shooter (or potential pass receiver/shooter) should be preparing his steps so that he is under control and balanced and can quickly execute the proper footwork once the ball is actually received. The "hands ready" part of the phrase simply means that the potential pass receiver/shooter should have both hands up to always be prepared to catch the ball and that the hands are already very close to the same position that they should be in when actually shooting the basketball. The hands are in the shooting pocket with both the shooting hand and the guide hand in almost the exact location they would be if the ball were actually in the offensive player's hands. Having the hands up and already in very close proximity to the shooting pocket also helps the passer out by giving him an exact target of where the receiver wants the ball passed to him. You should tell the pass receivers that their hand position helps make the passer a better passer (by giving the passer an excellent target, similar to a baseball catcher giving a target to a pitcher.) Shooters who want to get their shot off quicker (to avoid maximum defensive pressure) must have their feet and hands ready to receive the pass, then catch the ball, square up to the basket, and then shoot. For a shooter to be ready to shoot, the player must have the knowledge and skills to perform the proper pivots quickly in order to get his shoulders squared up and to get the shot off before an opposing defender can put more defensive pressure on him. In essence, the shooter must know how to create space and distance from his defender, whether off the dribble or off the pass. That important concept involves the proper footwork of the pass receiver/shooter.

Three Pivots of Shooters

Three different methods of pivoting successfully enable shooters to get their shot off quicker and therefore with less defensive pressure. A coach can teach all three methods, or he can limit his players to learning and developing one or two of these methods. Once the method has been chosen by the coaching staff, they should comprehensively present that method to the players. The reason that method is to be used should be thoroughly understood by both coaching staffs and players alike. The method should then be thoroughly taught and demonstrated to the players. The players should have numerous opportunities to practice the method with a close and positive scrutiny by the entire coaching staff.

One method could simply be called the two-step hop. As the ball is being passed to the shooter, the pass receiver/shooter takes a hop with both feet as he also squares up to the basket. Either foot becomes the actual pivot foot, and the shooter quickly becomes squared up to the basket as the pivot is made.

Another method that many coaches believe in is to teach every shooter to use a designated pivot foot, regardless of what side of the floor he is on. The strongpoint in this method is that it specializes each shooter into being very proficient in his pivoting (always off one specific foot) while catching the ball.

Another method of preparing to shoot the ball after receiving the pass is the pivoting off the inside foot method. This method requires pivoting off the foot that is the inside foot in relationship to the court. Shooters on the offense's left side of the court will use the right foot as the designated pivot foot when facing the basket and the left foot when their back is originally to the basket as they are about to receive the pass, and vice versa when the pass receiver/shooter is on the opposite side of the court.

Each shooter not only pivots off the inside foot, but the shooter pivots off the inside heel of the inside foot. Pivoting off the inside heel stops the momentum in the direction the potential shooter was going as a cutter (or dribbler). This momentum must be stopped so that the new momentum can be shifted to the direction of the basket. Allowing the original momentum to continue can cause the shooter to fall away from the basket after the shot or to drift to one side or the other during and after the shot.

All shooters should rise straight up and come straight down. If any landing occurs after the shot, it should be only falling slightly forward toward the target.

If the momentum of the initial cut was laterally to either the right or the left of the basket, or if the cut originated closer to the basket and continues out away from the basket, the momentum of those types of cuts must be completely stopped. This move can be done by the cutter (or dribbler) pivoting off the inside heel, immediately before the actual shot. Pivoting off the inside heel also allows for a simple, smooth, and easy pivot, which gets the shooter quickly squared up, facing the basket. In addition, the quick pivot gets the shooter's feet and legs directly below the body of the shooter.

An accurate shooter must be able to see the basket as soon as possible. Doing so enables the shooter to be more accurate. Proper footwork, which primarily involves the pivot, helps enable the shooter to see the basket sooner, as well as allowing him to release his shot much quicker.

Former NBA player Antoine Walker was once asked by ESPN about the techniques of his three-point shooting success. His answer was: First, "Get my feet set;" second, "Get my hands all ready to go;" and third, "Get my legs up under me." Using the (inside) heel pivot and having the hands up and ready can very much accomplish Antoine's NBA goal.

Shooter's Pivots Off Screens

Diagram 3-1 shows an example of a cutter (02) coming off a down screen (with his back initially toward the basket) while on the offense's left side of the court with the full intention of shooting after he receives the pass. He first will have to set his defender up before receiving the down screen that will free him up to take the shot off the pass. To do that, he will have to make a game-realistic V-cut by stepping into the lane with that inside foot. 02's initial inside foot (with his back to the basket) is his left foot. He then makes a change of direction by planting that inside foot, followed by a step with the right foot just prior to receiving the down screen.

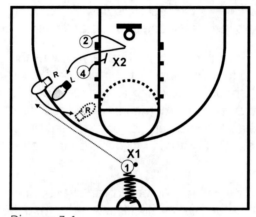

Diagram 3-1

After scraping off the down screen and getting open, he would then receive the pass. Upon receiving the pass, the potential perimeter jump shooter uses the left (inside) foot as the pivot foot. With his back to the basket, in this case the left foot is that inside foot. In this example, 04 is the down screener. 04 screens for 02 near the low post block. X4 still must guard 04 and will follow him as he sets the screen on X2. After setting the down screen, 04 can slip that screen and duck in to the middle of the lane to possibly become a greater scoring threat than 02 is on the perimeter. 04 will set the screen and either make a reverse pivot off his inside foot (which would be his right foot in this instance) to seal off his defender and post up near the lane, or 04 could make a forward (crossover) pivot with the same inside foot as the pivot foot. Both the original cutter and the screener must make the appropriate pivots, using the proper techniques to become viable scoring threats.

If a cutter is scraping off a down screen on the opposite side of the court, that cutter's initial inside foot and plant foot along with the down screener's inside foot and pivot foot would be the opposite feet respectively.

It must be noted that the following discussions and descriptions of V-cuts does not necessarily (and really should not) mean that a V-cut is just a single jab step. The

V-cut could be many more steps that are trying to sell the defenders that the offensive player is going in one direction further into or through the lane, when, in fact, the cutter is wanting to cut in the opposite direction. Three steps should be an adequate series of steps that could be described as the singular V-cut.

Diagram 3-2 shows a slightly different offensive action. In this case, O3 steps from the low post area (on the right side of the court) to set a (small-on-big) back screen on X5 for O5, who is initially facing the basket. O3 starts with his back to the basket. O3's inside foot (or pivot foot) is the right foot. After O5 makes a V-cut toward the middle of the floor to set his defender up, he should then plant the inside (left) foot before receiving the back screen. O5 then scrapes off of O3's back screen and cuts to the basket for a possible lob pass and high percentage shot.

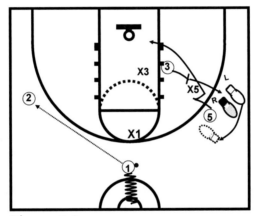

Diagram 3-2

The lob pass to the lob cutter is not the only offensive scoring threat. After setting the back screen, O3 can slip the screen and step out on the perimeter to become a potential passer/driver/shooter.

O3 uses the same type of footwork as if he were the offensive player to receive a down screen to get open on the perimeter, as previously discussed. He may feel he will become an instant jump shooter or could become just a passer/driver on the perimeter after slipping the back screen he set for O5. That decision most likely will affect what type of pivot O3 should use and which foot will be his actual pivot foot. In this situation, O3 front pivots off his initial right (inside) foot to become an immediate shooting threat. If he doesn't expect to be an immediate shooting threat, O3 could make a reverse pivot (which could be called an inside pivot since the pivot is actually towards the basket) off his outside foot (the left foot in this case). Upon catching the ball and pivoting in this manner, O3 is in triple-threat position, facing the basket. He now has his new inside foot as his pivot foot and his outside foot as the free foot (to drive toward the baseline on his particular side of the court).

Diagram 3-3 shows 04 setting a back flare screen for 02 on the offense's left side of the court. With 02 facing the basket, 02 sets his defender up by V-cutting toward the middle before then scraping off 04's flare screen toward the outside perimeter area. His V-cut will be executed by planting his right (inside) foot and then stepping out with his outside foot and cutting off of 04's screen to make his flare cut towards the left wing area. 02 remains somewhat facing the basket and the passer, before receiving the skip pass from 03. He can then become an immediate offensive triple threat by making a slight front pivot off his original inside (right) foot and swinging his free (left, in this situation) foot around to complete the full squaring up to the basket. Somewhat facing the skip passer and the basket allows for successful completion of the pass as well as being able to get the shot off even more quickly from the skip pass.

The flare screener (04) starts with his back to the basket. After setting his screen, 04 can slip the screen by popping out on the perimeter or by stepping into the lane toward the ball. If he feels he can get an immediate shot off the pass, 04 slips the flare screen and cuts toward the ball. If he receives the pass, he should front pivot off his inside foot (the left foot from the left side of the court and with his back to the basket) to square up for an immediate jump shot near the elbow area.

Diagram 3-4 illustrates various types of offensive action, including V-cuts, screens, slipping of screens, and different types of pivots. 01 makes a pass to 02, who has freed himself from his defender. 02 has made an exaggerated V-cut to get open at the free throw line extended. 02 starts by facing the basket and makes a backdoor cut before planting his outside (left) foot and pushes off with that same foot. He uses his inside (right) foot to pop out back to his original area. When 02 catches the ball with his back to the basket, he must quickly decide if he is going to be a potential shooter or passer/ driver. This decision will dictate which type of pivot and which foot will be the pivot foot, as has been previously discussed.

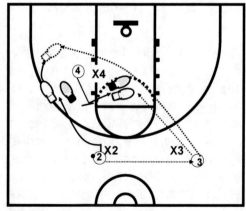

Diagram 3-3

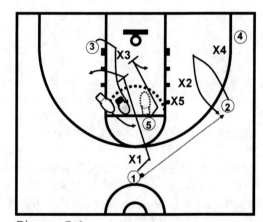

Diagram 3-4

03 starts on the offense's left mid-post block area with his back to the basket and is going to receive a stagger screen from 05 and the original passer (01). This stagger screen should free 03 from his defender, X3. 03 wants to get open near the top of the key for a jump shot with minimal defensive pressure.

To free himself of his defender, 03 must also make a strong V-cut to set his defender up even before the stagger screen action (of 05 and 01) begins. 03 would plant his inside foot (left in this case) and then step up to receive the stagger screens set by teammates 01 and 05 (as the outside screener and the inside screener respectively) with his right foot. The front pivot versus the reverse pivot allows 03 to be able to always see all four important pieces of the offensive action: the passer with the basketball, the two stagger screeners, and his defender.

When a stagger screen is set, it is most likely that the cutter receiving the screen should have an open shot opportunity somewhere on the perimeter. 03 should scrape off the screen and prepare himself for the quick shot off the pass by getting his feet and hands ready.

Diagram 3-5 shows the actual footwork of the cutter (03) as well as both screeners (01 and 05) in the stagger screen action. This footwork entails that 03 pivot off his inside (left) heel as he scrapes off 01's outside shoulder and peeks around the stagger screen to receive the basketball from 02. Scraping off the screen and cutting toward the passer helps prepare 03 for more successfully receiving the pass as well as shooting more quickly off the screens and therefore greatly reducing the amount of defensive pressure on his shot.

03 is not the only offensive player using various types of pivots in this action. In Diagram 3-5, 01 reverse pivots off the foot farthest from the ball and drifts out of the lane. The reverse pivot allows 01 to maintain sight of the ball and the passer (02), the

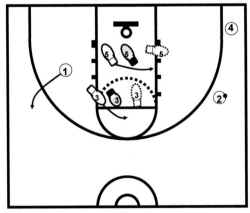

Diagram 3-5

cutter (03) and the second screener (05). The second screener, the inside screener (05), also makes a reverse pivot off the foot closest to the ball (the right foot in this case), opens up to the ball and steps back toward the basketball. In this pivot, 05 picks up sight of the ball earlier as he cuts toward the ball and the middle of the free throw lane.

Diagram 3-6 shows a ball screen set by 04 for 01. 01 scrapes off the outside shoulder of 04 to the right wing area. After setting the ball screen, 04 rolls to the basket. 04 could possibly set the ball screen before then receiving a screen-the-screener screen-and-lob cut to the basket, or he could possibly then receive a flare screen followed by his flare cut to the wide wing area, or he could simply slip his ball screen and remain outside as a perimeter player in what can be called pick-and-pop action. 04 slips the screen and stay outside of the three-point line as a potential offensive triple threat. The proper footwork for 04 to use in the pick-and-pop action is to reverse pivot (off the inside foot) so that he can more easily maintain sight of the ball, the basket, and his defender before receiving the potential throwback pass.

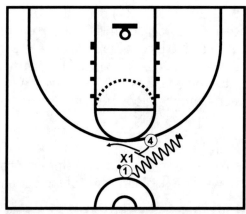

Diagram 3-6

Diagrams 3-7 and 3-8 show 02 coming off screens while initially facing the basket. In both instances, 02 must utilize a front pivot with the inside pivot foot (right foot) to square up to the basket as a potential shooter or passer.

Diagram 3-7 shows the action of a flare screen set by 05 for 02 so that 01 can make a skip pass to 02 on the weakside wing area. Since 02 has stayed mainly facing the basket, he should pivot off his inside heel (the right heel) and make the short swing of his free foot (left) to completely square up to the basket to be able to more quickly shoot off the skip pass.

The flare screener (05) could also be a secondary scoring threat after slipping his flare screen by simply stepping toward the ball. Initially with his back to the basket, 05 could then make a front pivot off his inside (left) foot as he catches the pass from 01 to attack his defender.

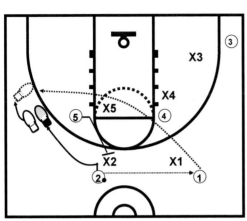

Diagram 3-7

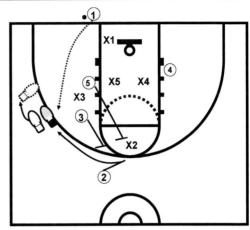

Diagram 3-8

Diagram 3-8 shows a typical baseline out-of-bounds play with 03 receiving screens on the offensive left side of the court. 02 sets up his defender with a V-cut before cutting toward the screener. The V-cut begins with a step with the inside foot (right) before using a front crossover step as he scrapes off the screen (set by 05 and 03, respectively). In both cases, at the moment of catching the ball, 02 would make a front pivot off the inside (right) heel and swing the outside free foot (left) around to square up to the basket. This move allows 02 to quickly take a shot immediately off the inbounds pass from 01.

Diagram 3-9 shows 02 on the left side of the court coming off a double screen while somewhat facing both the basket and the ball (in 03's hands on the right side of the floor). 02 cuts off the double screen into the lane as he looks to receive the ball from 03, who is located near the free throw line extended on the right side of the court. To set his defender (X2) up, 02 must first make a V-cut by stepping toward the basket, planting his left foot as the pivot foot, and then making a front crossover step to

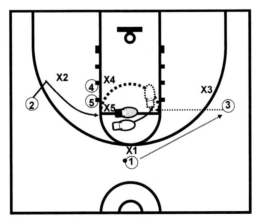

Diagram 3-9

scrape off the top screener's (O5) high shoulder. O2 cuts across the lane and prepares his feet and hands to receive the pass from O3. If he feels he will have an open jump shot immediately off the pass, he would plant and pivot off his inside heel (left foot) before swinging his outside foot (right) to square up and quickly get his jump shot off.

The same overall offensive technique for the cutters/shooters should again be used to get the feet and hands ready. If either screener (O4 or O5) sees his defender trying to switch or hedge on the cutter, he could slip the screen and step toward the ball and into the lane, while also getting his feet and hands ready. If he is facing the original cutter (O2) toward the outside, he would have to reverse pivot with the contact foot (the foot closest to their defender) to effectively seal off the defender.

In this example, X5 is playing on the top side of his man. O5 would have to reverse pivot, using his top foot as the contact foot and therefore the pivot foot. O5 would swing his right foot into X5 and seal X5 off, with his hands up while looking for the basketball from O3 as he steps farther into the lane. X4 is playing on the low side of O4, which dictates that O4 make a reverse pivot off his right (low) foot and swing his left foot into X4 to seal off his defender. His hands ought to be ready also.

Diagram 3-10 is an example of O2 setting a ball screen for O1, receiving a back/flare screen from O4, and then receiving a skip pass from O1 on the right side of the offense. This screen is the traditional pick-the-picker action, with the new cutter/shooter (O2) facing the basket (on the offense's right side of the court).

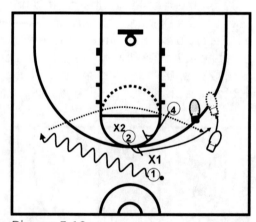

Diagram 3-10

Diagram 3-10 has O2 facing the offense's right sideline while aligned at the top of the key, and then setting the ball screen for O1 to dribble scrape off as he heads to the free throw line extended on the offense's left side. O4 steps up to set a flare screen for O2 to make a flare cut to the free throw line extended on the right side of the court. As O2 scrapes off O4's flare screen and flare cuts, he should already start to square his shoulders up to the basket. O2 starts to face the basket as well as look over his inside (left, in this case) shoulder for the passer (either 01 or 04). 02's footwork should be the same as any potential shooter that is facing the basket on the right side of the court. 02 should pivot off his inside (left) heel and make a front pivot with his outside (right) foot to square up and become an immediate offensive triple threat when he receives the skip pass.

Pivots Used in Stationary Shooting (Facing the Basket)

The only exception to the "inside foot is the pivot foot" rule for all prospective shooters off the pass is the stationary shooter who is already facing his basket, particularly in zone offenses and sometimes in specific man offenses. If the stationary shooter has a distinct preference in having a specific foot as the pivot foot, coaches could allow the shooter to use that favorite pivot foot. Most right-handed shooters prefer to use the left foot as the pivot foot, while, conversely, the majority of left-handed shooters like to use the right foot as the pivot foot.

Diagram 3-11 illustrates a right-handed shooter, setting up in a stationary position, on the left wing in a half-court offensive set. If this right-handed shooter has a strong preference of using the left foot as the pivot foot, the shooter lines up with the left foot as the pivot foot, slightly ahead of the right foot. The player's right foot opens up to face the point guard, with the pivot foot (left) facing the basket, while the hands are already in position to catch (and immediately shoot off the catch). As the ball is caught, the heel of the left pivot foot touches the floor. The right foot steps up, and the ball is immediately pulled into the shooting pocket. The shot can be taken more quickly and therefore with less defensive resistance if all of the proper (feet and hand preparation) fundamentals and techniques are utilized. Less defensive pressure makes the chance of scoring off this shot more likely to be successful.

Diagram 3-11

Diagram 3-12 shows the same half-court offensive scenario, but on the offense's right side of the court. The right-handed pass receiver lines his feet up with the left foot again as the pivot foot and slightly ahead of the right (free) foot. The pass receiver has already started squaring his shoulders up toward the basket and has his hands up and ready (to catch and shoot instantly off the pass.). This technique allows the shooter more time to get the shot off with less defensive pressure.

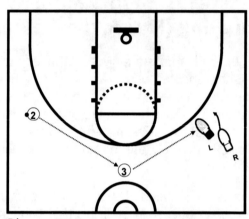

Diagram 3-12

Going back to the offensive left side of the court, Diagram 3-13 illustrates a half-court left-handed shooter who prefers to use the right foot as the pivot foot. Being in a stationary position, the half-court offensive player starts his initial position of facing the basket even before the pass is made. The right foot is the favored pivot foot and starts slightly ahead of the left foot. That inside (right) foot that is to be the pivot foot is already facing the basket. Both hands are turned toward the passer. Both hands are already positioned so that as soon as the ball is caught, the hands can bring the ball back into the shooting pocket and immediately shoot the ball. Again, this technique

Diagram 3-13

should make the passer a more accurate passer now that he has a specific target to pass the ball to. This pivot should help the shooter get his shot off more quickly, which is a great advantage to the shooter.

Diagram 3-14 illustrates the left-handed shooter on the right side of the court, still favoring using the right foot as the pivot foot. In this half-court offense, the pass receiver/shooter can set up with the pivot foot already facing the basket and the free (left) foot somewhat facing the passer. The hands are facing the passer, again presenting the passer with a very good passing target. When the ball is caught, the ball is simultaneously brought into the shooting pocket as the free foot is brought slightly forward to square the shoulders and facing the basket.

Coaches should only allow shooters this exception to the rule of pivoting off the inside foot when the shooter has a very strong preference. This exception should occur only when in a half-court offense with stationary prospective shooters, in zone or man offenses.

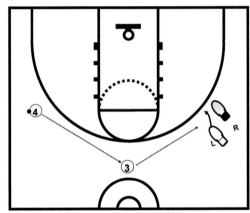

Diagram 3-14

Shooting Off the Move: Cutting or Dribbling

Shooting off a dribble or shooting off a pass that is preceded by a cut are both shooting off the move. When a shooter shoots the ball off the dribble, coaches should use the same concepts, methods, techniques, and coaching/teaching phrases as when the shooter is receiving the pass and then quickly shooting the ball off a cut. The timing and positioning of the feet and hands should be almost identical, while the rhythm should also be the same. The dribblers or cutters should stay balanced as they are moving and they should be a quick as they can be without losing the all-important balance and body control factors. As Coach John Wooden always preaches, "Be quick, but not in a hurry."

If a dribbler is on the left side of the court dribbling toward the basket, the dribbler must dribble with the outside (left) hand that is the farthest from the defender. When coming to a stop, the dribbler pivots off the inside heel of the inside foot. This pivot is done for the same reasons as a cutter/pass receiver that is breaking to an open spot on the right side of the court. Utilizing the heel of the inside foot immediately stops the lateral momentum of the dribbler, which allows the shooter to rise straight up and come back down in almost the same spot where he took off. If a shooter does not land where he has launched, a shooter's accuracy will greatly decrease. Good shooters do not fall away or float either to the left or to the right

The dribbler makes the last dribble before the shot the lowest and the hardest dribble of all of his dribbles. This technique helps generate momentum for the shooter's actual takeoff or launch for the jump shot. The hands should be in a very similar proximity as if the shooter were catching the basketball from a teammate's pass. The rhythm and fluidity of getting both hands quickly and easily into the shooting pocket should be nearly identical for a potential shooter in both the pass receiving and the dribbling scenarios. The closer the two similarities are in the two scenarios, the better the shooter will be in both facets—shooting off the pass and shooting off the dribble.

Diagram 3-15 shows a dribbler dribbling to his left. This approach makes the outside hand (away from the defender) the left hand, while the inside foot is the right foot. The heel of the inside foot should drive itself straight down hard into the floor at the exact time that the last dribble hits the floor. This technique is identical in what should be taught for a cutter that is receiving the pass and instantly shooting off the pass. The cutter/shooter should drive his inside heel down the moment the ball is hitting his shooting (target) hand. The left (free) foot should swing around to finish squaring up the shoulders as the ball is pulled into the shooting pocket with both the shooting hand and the guide hand as the shooter begins his jump.

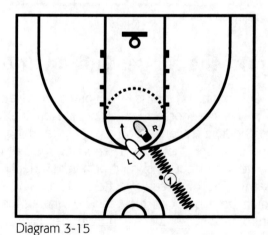

Diagram 3-15

Diagram 3-16 displays a dribbler dribbling to his right. This approach makes the outside hand (away from the defender) the right hand, while the inside foot or the pivot foot is now the left foot. As the last dribble is made, the left heel should be driving down to again stop the lateral offensive momentum of the potential shooter. As the ball is pulled into the shooting pocket, the free (right) foot swings around to face the basket (to square up for the shot) and is quickly followed by the actual jumping by the shooter.

Diagram 3-16

Breakdown Pivoting Drills for Shooters

To improve the footwork (and the handwork) of the shooters, it is imperative that a coaching staff has several breakdown drills that deal with nothing but the proper footwork needed for a good shooter to be successful. Later, other drills involving the actual shooting of the ball can be incorporated.

To make these breakdown drills more time-efficient and to get more receivers/shooters involved in the drills simultaneously, coaches could have the pass receivers pass the ball to themselves by tossing the ball slightly out in front of them. To concentrate on nothing but the footwork (and handwork) off the pass, coaches could have the pass receivers/shooters toss the ball to themselves but not actually shoot the ball (at a basket). This approach allows the players to focus on what the staff wants them to concentrate on as well as save valuable practice time. The actual shooting of the ball will not be a distraction or consume valuable time, when the time is solely spent on executing the proper footwork and handwork for potential shooters off the pass.

After the receivers/shooters catch the pass (from themselves), each shooter should pivot off the inside foot, square up (to an imaginary basket), and stop. By not shooting the ball, a tremendous amount of time is saved and no distractions are made.

By using the circles at a possible six free throw lines and the center jump circle in a typical gymnasium, visual references and guides for each and every drill participant is available.

Three or four players can set up at each of these seven locations. The players can be instructed to jog under control in a clockwise direction slightly outside the line of the circle. A ball, a manager, or a coach can be positioned in the exact center of each circle to represent a hypothetical passer with the ball. This central location puts the hypothetical passer in the same position and location regardless of where the various cutters/potential pass receivers/potential shooters are on the circle. Also, a coach in the center of a circle can clearly see the footwork of every player in the specific group. The players on a command are told to start their jogging around their circle. On a second command, each player stops the jog and tosses the ball slightly ahead of himself. He then pivots off the heel of the inside foot as he catches the pass (from himself), pulls the ball into his shooting pocket and squares up to the (simulated) basket located in the center of the circle.

On the next command, all four players start their jog again until they again hear the next command to pivot and square up. After several repetitions, each group of four players switches the clockwise direction of their jogging. Jogging counterclockwise around the circle forces each shooter to now use the left foot as the new inside pivot foot.

Diagram 3-17 shows 01, 02, 03, and 04 using one of the circles jogging in a clockwise direction and working on the proper footwork and handwork off the simulated pass. In this clockwise direction, all four potential pass receivers/shooters should be around the circle under control ready to catch the pass (from themselves). On the whistle, all four cutters toss their basketball out in front of them to catch the pass (from themselves). As they catch the pass, each should make a quick but under control front pivot off the inside (right) heel to completely square up to the (imaginary) basket in the center of the circle. They swing their free foot (left) around and take the shot at the center of the circle.

As shown in Diagram 3-18, this same format of the footwork drill can also be used for dribblers/shooters, because the basic footwork (and handwork) techniques for all cutters/shooters are the same as for all dribblers/shooters. In this same clockwise direction, all four dribblers should be dribbling with their head up under control and using their outside (left) hand. On the whistle, all four dribblers pivot off their inside (right) heel and make a front pivot to square up to the (imaginary) basket in the center of the circle. They swing their free foot (left) around and take the shot to the imaginary basket, located at the center of the circle.

To make sure all players can shoot while cutting or dribbling from their left or their right, these two drills should be used by going in both directions. Players like to work on drills where they are already fundamentally strong, but coaches must motivate players to work on skills and techniques where the players show weaknesses and, therefore, must improve those techniques.

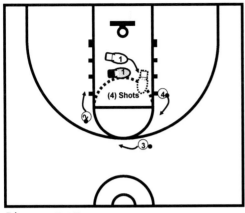

Diagram 3-17

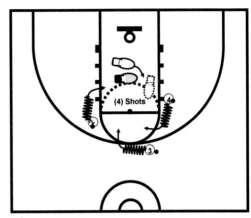

Diagram 3-18

Diagram 3-19 illustrates 05, 06, 07, and 08 starting at a different circle and going in a counterclockwise direction. These players dribble with the outside hand (right hand) and go around the circle. On a command, they kill their dribble as they pivot off the heel of the inside foot (left) to square up to the simulated basket. On the next command, the four players start dribbling awaiting the next signal to pivot off the inside heel and square up again.

Diagram 3-20 illustrates the same players practicing their shooting footwork (and handwork) techniques going in the same counterclockwise direction, but this time off the pass. Again, the same techniques should be used, and the same timing and rhythm should be emphasized.

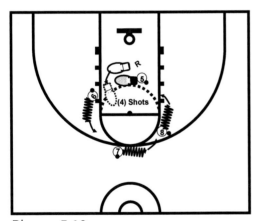

Diagram 3-19

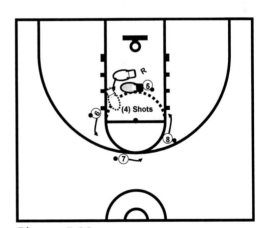

Diagram 3-20

Cutting, Outlet Pass, and Shooting Drill

A drill emphasizing proper footwork and handwork of both cutters/shooters and rebounders, in addition to the actual shooting and outlet passing of the basketball is described in the following section. Diagram 3-21 shows four pairs of players at each basket. Each player in the lane passes the ball to his cutting teammate on the perimeter (the first session in front of the three-point line, and the second session behind the three-point line). Each cutter starts by facing the basket and cutting to his right, getting his feet and hands ready to catch and shoot. This positioning makes each cutter's inside foot to be the left foot, which will be the pivot foot as the pass is received. As the ball is actually caught, the heel of the inside foot should be driven down and the outside free foot (right) swings around to square up the shooter's shoulders before the shot is taken.

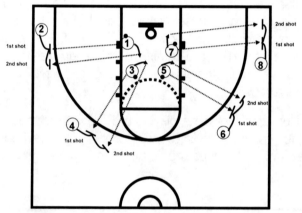

Diagram 3-21

After the shot, the passing teammate rebounds the shot, while the shooting teammate again gets his feet and hands ready. The rebounders can also work on reading the trajectory of the shot and the proper techniques of rebounding the basketball. The rebounder (now the outlet passer) can work on the proper techniques of pivoting off his outside foot and making a front pivot (away from the imaginary opponent), swinging his inside foot around before making a two-hand overhead outlet pass to a teammate in the drill (see Chapter 5).

When the rebounder secures the rebound, the cutter starts the next cut in the same direction, and the rebounder passes the ball again to the cutting shooter. The cutting shooter continues the rotation around the perimeter of the court until he gets the deep corner spot, where he runs out-of-bounds. Afterwards, the cutter should sprint across the baseline and start in the deep corner on the opposite side of the floor. After a designated number of shots, the passing rebounders switch positions with the cutting shooters.

After both players in the two-man group have executed the drill, the drill can then be repeated in the same direction, but with the cutting shooters not shooting immediately off the pass. Instead, the cutter/shooter catches the ball, shot fakes, and then dribbles one or two dribbles before actually shooting off the dribble. The cutter/dribbler/shooter uses the same techniques, pivoting off the heel of the inside foot, swinging the free foot around to square up the shoulders, and shooting the basketball with a fundamentally sound follow-through.

This drill also can be run for pass receivers/shooters or for cutters/shooters going in either a clockwise or a counterclockwise direction. The third variation of this drill could be for players to execute a game-realistic shot fake, before dribbling a required number of times before shooting.

Individual, group, and team goals could be established when these drills are executed, so that each drill offers pressure and competition. This approach makes the drills more exciting, less mundane for the players, as well as more game realistic and, therefore, more productive for all involved.

Summary

Teaching the proper footwork and handwork for all offensive players and then closely observing, critiquing, and correcting those players during specific breakdown drills will allow those players to become more proficient in all of the important shooting fundamentals and techniques. This approach will give players a much greater opportunity to succeed while shooting the ball. Having proper mechanics and techniques for all shooters cannot be minimized and taken lightly.

As important as shooting is to the overall offensive schemes of a basketball team, the art of pivoting is just as important. Pivoting is an integral part of rebounding, passing, getting open to receive a pass, pass receiving, and overall shooting techniques. The art of pivoting is essential to the overall offensive success of a basketball team.

4

Important Pivots of the Offensive Post Player

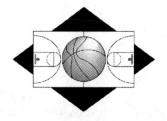

*"Footwork and balance are
necessary every moment of a game."*
—Coach Pete Newell

Many basketball coaches believe that going inside on offense is one of the most important concepts of offensive basketball. Going inside allows an offensive team greater opportunities for close high percentage shots. Going inside allows an offense greater opportunities to draw fouls, thereby shooting more free throws. It also places the opponents' defensive players into potential foul trouble, thereby reducing opposing players playing time and their offensive scoring contributions, their rebounding, and their defensive post play. Going inside can very likely also set up an outside game, giving the offensive team a more well-balanced and more difficult offense that can that can attack the opposition's defense.

Passing the ball inside requires several different pivoting techniques. For pass receivers, it is extremely important in initiating the process of scoring points in the paint for post players to possess the skills needed to get open against aggressive post defenders. But getting open inside followed by the pass inside still doesn't produce points for the offense.

The actual scoring of points requires the final series of offensive techniques and proper footwork. Sound fundamental footwork in the offensive post game is necessary for getting open, creating space, and getting the shot off. Footwork helps produces points.

Offensive post moves with the ball are the final key to offensive scoring success in the low-post area. What sometimes is forgotten is how important the art of pivoting is to the offensive moves of a post player.

Offensive post players can be played defensively in a variety of ways. An offensive counter-attack must be in place for each of those defensive methods. If not successful, every opponent will learn from the success of prior opponents and apply that same method. The offensive inside game's production will soon dwindle. Without inside and outside balance, before long, the offensive perimeter game also will suffer, and reduction in overall team performance will soon follow.

Getting Open

Footwork for an offensive post player (as well as for a defensive post player) is essential for the overall success of those offensive players. An offensive post player must get open before he can receive the ball, and that post player must have possession of the ball before he can score or draw fouls on the opposition.

Coaches could use the phrase *the battle of the feet* in describing how the offensive post player must position his feet (and body) to make himself available to receive the pass. Coaching staffs can also say to all (offensive as well as defensive) post players, "You can't win the war unless you win the battle." This instruction tells interior players that without proper footwork techniques, they will not be able to receive the ball. If they don't receive the ball, they cannot score.

The quickest and simplest way to get good offensive position on a post defender is to beat that opponent down the floor. Post players should hustle to beat their defender to the spot just above the low block, establish that position, and then maintain that position on the side of the lane. That position is a spot no lower than the first notch above the block.

One effective way an offense can score points is for the offensive post players to score on the interior. For post players to score inside, they must be able to operate effectively first without and then with the ball against numerous types of defenses. For post players with the ball to be able to attack the defense and score, they must first know how to get open. Against a strong and aggressive defense, the post player may have to utilize specific moves to get open as they try to receive an inside pass.

Two Individual Techniques to Get Open

Against a good defense, a post player cannot just flash to the ball and expect to receive the ball where he wants it. Following are some individual moves that all offensive post players should be able to learn and use to be effective offensive post players.

These individual offensive moves without the ball to free themselves from their defender work just as well for players on the perimeter that face aggressive denial defensive pressure. One method of getting open where a player wants to get open is called the rip move, another is called the swim move, while another technique is called the contact and reverse pivot move.

These individual post techniques require pivots and other strong footwork by the flash post players. These moves first include a two- or three-step V-cut before the actual flash across the lane to the basketball.

If the defender (X5) has started playing the offensive player (O5) low, O5 should take his defender lower. A V-cut (that could ideally consist of one or more initial steps) in one direction (low) followed by a cut in the opposite direction (high) should be executed by using a front pivot.

Diagrams 4-1 and 4-2 illustrate one of the two types of V-cuts, one faking low and cutting high. With his back to the basket, O5 can see his teammates, his defender (X5), and how he is being played. He also knows the location of the ball. All of these elements factor in the moves and techniques that the offensive player should utilize.

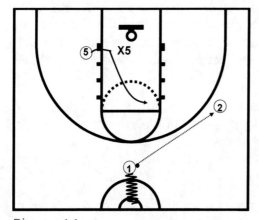

Diagram 4-1

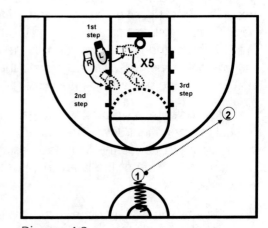

Diagram 4-2

With the post player (O5) on the offense's left side of the free throw lane and his back to the basket, O5 first makes his V-cut by planting his inside (left) foot in the lane, followed by a step with his right foot and then crossing over in somewhat of a front crossover pivot (with his left foot) before flashing across the lane toward the basketball on the opposite side of the court. When the front crossover pivot is being made, the offensive post player should rip with the contact arm (the left arm, in this case) across the defender's chest and scrape off of his defender as he flashes to the ball across the lane. This move gives the defender no spacing for a proper angle of pursuit to catch up to or to cut off the flash post cut of the offensive player.

Diagrams 4-3 and 4-4 illustrate another type of V-cut, starting with a fake high and cut low across the lane to chase the basketball. Diagram 4-3 illustrates 05 again preparing to flash to the ball against his defender (X5). In this situation, 05 should read that X5 is playing him high, so 05 should start with a high V-cut, before then cutting low. The first step in this case should be with the top (right) foot higher, then with the lower (left) foot, and then with a front crossover step with the top (right) foot. As the front crossover step is being made, the post player should again rip the contact arm (this time, it is the right arm) past the defender's baseline shoulder as he cuts low across the lane to post up on the opposite side of the lane. He should remember to post up on the notch above the block and then hold his ground.

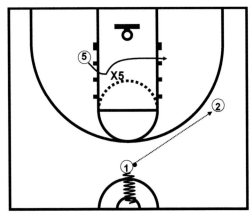

Diagram 4-3

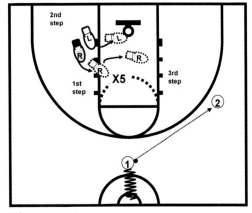

Diagram 4-4

Good post defenders will know where offensive post players want to go, and they will attempt to prevent an offensive player from going to those desired locations. The concept and the short teaching phrase coaches should use to simplify the teaching process is as follows:

Concept: "If you are stationary in the post area and the defense plays you on the low side, start your initial positioning in the post by originally setting up lower."

Teaching phrase: "If they start low, you start lower. (But never start below the block.)"

Concept: "If the stationary situation has the defender playing you on the high side, start your positioning higher."

Teaching phrase: "If they start high, you start higher."

Concept: "If the defender tries to takes the low cut away, first take him lower and then make the flash post cut toward the high side."

Teaching phrase: "If they play you low, take them lower and scrape cut high."

Concept: "If the post defender tries to take the high cut away, first take the defender higher then make the flash post cut toward the low side."

Teaching phrase: "If they play you high, take them higher and scrape cut low."

Swim Move

Offensive and defensive post play can be a very physical part of the game and both offensive and defensive post players have to learn the techniques of legal physical post play. If the defender (X5) tries physically to deny the offensive flash cuts by 05 by hugging up on the post player and playing him much tighter, 05 needs to make a somewhat similar move to be able to neutralize the more physical play of X5. The same phrases previously taught can be used, but with one word (swim) added to each of the phrases.

After V-cutting, if X5 tries to jam 05's cut by being physical, 05 might have to swing his contact arm over the defender as he is making his front crossover step because no space is available to rip his arm through the defender. These swim move concepts and techniques and teaching phrases are as follows:

Concept: "If the defender jams the low cut away, first take him lower, and then swim to make the flash post cut toward the high side."

Teaching phrase: "If they jam you low, take them lower and swim high."

Concept: "If the post defender jams the high cut away, first take him higher, and then swim to make the flash post cut toward the low side."

Teaching phrase: "If they jam you high, take them higher and swim low."

Concept: "A key point for the flash cutter is to get as close to the defender before making the front (pivot) crossover move to get open."

Teaching phrase: "Get into the defender's body before you make your swim move."

The swim technique of the arms added to the front crossover step footwork neutralizes the defender's more aggressive action. The offensive post player should end up in the location where he wants to go. This swim technique takes advantage of the aggressiveness and the strong defensive action.

In Diagram 4-5, the defender (X4) is shaded more on the flash cutter's right side (whose back is toward the basket), so the left (higher) foot of the flash post player (04) is the free foot that makes the first step toward the defender to get closer to the defender. Getting closer to the defender will eventually give that defender less reaction time when the offensive player makes the actual cut he wants to make to actually get open. The second step is with the right foot into the lane as 04 makes a front crossover pivot move (with the right foot swinging over/through the defender).

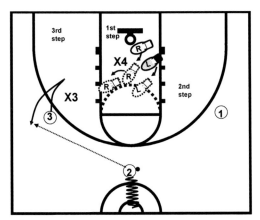

Diagram 4-5

At the same time of the front crossover step, 04 should swing his contact arm over the defender to avoid the contact and the legal bumping technique by any defender who is defending and denying any offensive player from receiving the basketball (whether on the interior or on the perimeter.) This effective move, called a swim move is used to "swim" over the defender that now has very close proximity to the offensive post player. The swim move allows the offensive cutter to free himself from the defender and ultimately end up on the high side of the defender and actually closer to the ball than the actual defender.

Keep in mind that the swim move is just as effective on the perimeter as well as in post area. In Diagram 4-5, 03 would start by facing the basket and should make a V-cut toward the basket with his right foot (contact foot) first and then a front crossover step with his left foot before then executing a swim move on his defender (X3). Here, the swim move is used to get between his defender and the ball to then get open to receive the initial wing pass from 01.

Contact and Reverse Pivot Move

The second individual move is called the contact and reverse pivot move. Diagram 4-6 illustrates this individual move. All offensive personnel are in the same locations as in Diagram 4-5. In this scenario, 02 reverses the ball to 01, who swings the ball around the perimeter to the opposite side of the court to 03. X4 prevents the duck-in cut of 04 by playing on the high side of 04. X4 attempts to defend 04's duck-in cut, by using physical contact to jam the duck-in cut. 04 steps into the body of X4 by placing his contact foot (which is the lower baseline foot or his right foot, in this case) between the two feet of X4 and then make a strong and quick reverse pivot by swinging his left foot toward the baseline while holding his left arm and elbow up as an arm bar. He should then be on the low (baseline) side of X4. He seals X4 off with his high foot (the left, in this instance) and arm/elbow. The arm bar should stay up and 04 should try to sit down

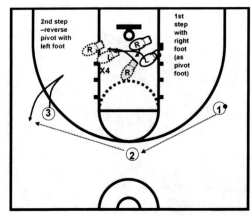

Diagram 4-6

on X4's low leg (right leg, in this case). O4 wants to stay on or above the first notch above the block to have the very best angle to be able to drop-step toward the basket by going to his left or to his right. Note that O3 might have to step toward the basket before utilizing the same footwork and reverse pivot to get open on the perimeter to become the passer to his teammate now posting up on his side of the lane.

Spin Screen Move

Most modern offensive schemes desire all players to eventually end up in the post area as well as the perimeter area. A third technique requires a teammate to help out the offensive post player. This third technique may be the most devastating method that a post player can use to receive the ball where he wants the ball: in the lane for maximum scoring opportunities.

This third move, called the spin screen move, seems to be almost unbeatable, but it requires two players: the original ballside post player (05, in this case) and a teammate to set a screen for him. This screen is basically an interior back screen with a weakside post player (02, in this example) setting a spin (back) screen when the ball is reversed on the perimeter to the top of the key. Ideally, if a smaller offensive teammate is the actual spin screener, it can be advantageous for the offense.

This mismatch in size between the actual screener (02) and the spin screen cutter (05, in this case) discourages defensive switches when the ball is reversed to the center of the court. If a defense switches the small-on-big spin screen, the smaller (more likely weaker and less skilled post defender) will be forced to defend the big offensive post player in the paint. Minimal (if any) interior defensive support would result because of spacing on the perimeter as well as having the ball in the center of the floor, which means no true ballside and no true helpside exist, and the closest defenders not involved in the two-man screening action are on both perimeter wing areas at the free throw line extended.

Diagram 4-7 displays the original ballside post player (05) looking to receive the ball from 01 on the ballside wing. 02 starts in the weakside post area, 04 is the weakside wing, and 03 is at the top of the key. When the ball is reversed from 01 to 03, the (original) ballside low post (05) makes a normal duck-in cut to the center of the lane just inside the (old) dotted circle line. This form of attack is aggressive and normal for an offensive post player.

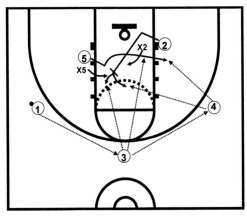

Diagram 4-7

If X5 plays behind 05's original duck-in cut, 05 should be able to receive the ball from 03 in an ideal scoring location. If X5 jams the duck-in cut, 05 could use the proper footwork to make what can be called the spin cut, which is basically the contact and reverse pivot move with one major exception. 05 will have the added advantage of 02 coming across the lane and head hunting X5 with a blind back screen. If X5 jams 05 on his duck-in cut, 05 then reverse pivots and cuts low, and he should scrape off of the (small-on-big) lane exchange back screen set by 02 on the low (baseline) side of the spin screen.

The weakside post player (02) should originally start on a lower vertical level than 05. This level places 02 out of the line of sight of X5, giving 02 a better screening angle to aggressively blindside 05's defender with a (in this case, small-on-big) back screen. X5 should have placed all of his attention and effort on defending 05's duck-in cut. When 05 gets jammed by X5, he changes direction and uses the reverse pivot, and it will seem that 02 came out of nowhere to blindside X5 on the almost indefensible back screen.

If X5 and X2 elect to switch the spin screen, X2 will end up having to attempt to defend 05 (which could be a huge height mismatch) on the opposite side of the court from where 05 started, but this defensive switch will also give the offense a second high potential scoring threat. If 02 sets the spin screen on X5 and the defense switches that screen, 02 would be on the inside half of X5 in the middle of the lane. If 02 then seals his new defender (X5), he will most likely become a second viable scoring threat off the spin screen action with very good offensive positioning. If 02 has had the proper offensive post moves training and education, he may actually be the primary scoring threat on this offensive action.

Diagram 4-8 illustrates the precise footwork of the spin screen cutter (05), originally lined up on the offense's left low-post block when the ball is reversed to the top of the key. 05 would start his duck-in cut with the first step being with his inside contact foot (left foot with his back to the basket and on the offense's left side of the court). He would follow with the normal right foot if his defender didn't deny the cut. But when X5 denies the pass by three-quarter or full fronting the duck-in cut, 02 cuts across the lane and sets the spin screen. 05's next step with the right foot is a reverse pivot spinning off the low (baseline) shoulder of the spin screener, 02. 05 reverse pivots and spins a complete 180 degrees off of 02 and cuts across the lane to post up on the opposite side of the lane.

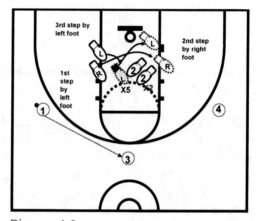

Diagram 4-8

Because the defender would have to make contact with the cutter's left side, 05's right foot is the free foot that makes the spin move. 05 spins around to the baseline side of the defender to ultimately free himself from either defender.

05 places the contact foot (the foot that is on the side closest to his defender) in between the two feet of that defender and uses that foot as the pivot foot. After stepping into X5, 05 then makes a 180-degree reverse pivot and swings the free foot (right foot, in this instance) around the defender to seal off that defender, regardless of whether the defender is X5 or is now X2.

The elbow (right) that is on the same side as the free foot (the free elbow) is to be held high and locked as the reverse pivot is made, similar to the reverse pivot made when executing defensive box-outs. When the free foot (right foot) swings around the defender, the post player should hold off the defender by using the free elbow. He should also use his backside, making contact with the defender and holding the contact. The post player should sit down on the (left) leg of the defender to keep him sealed off. Coaches should use the phrase, *It is a battle of the feet.* "To win the war (catch and score), the battle (of the feet) must be won." It doesn't matter which defender attempts to guard the post player (O5) when he posts up on the opposite side of the lane, but it is extremely important that O5 does not allow the defender to push him below the new ballside block. The ideal location would be for O5 to try to establish and maintain his new location on the notch above the block (for maximum scoring opportunities).

Obviously, if the offensive post player starts on the opposite side of the court (while making a V-cut and faking low to go high, or making a V-cut and faking high to go low, making a swim move to get open, or making a spin move to get open), the footwork would be the same, but using the opposite foot that is shown in Diagrams 4-4, 4-5, and 4-8.

Diagram 4-7 first displays O5 making the proper duck-in cut followed by the spin move off O2's screen with X5 and X2 switching that screen. O2 sets the screen on X5's backside as he would always do. X2 switches this spin screen in an attempt to deny the primary pass receiver/scorer (O5) from receiving the pass. If the defensive opponents make a switch on the spin screen action, two highly probable scoring threats result—both the spin screen cutter (O5) and the actual spin screener (O2). The primary receiver could vary every time this spin screen action is run. The offense could look for a specific offensive player inside to be the primary scoring threat, could look to attack a specific defensive opponent, or could have a completely open mind and simply look for the offensive player that is more open. These options that the spin screen action possesses make this offensive action even more difficult to defend because of its increased level of unpredictability.

Diagrams 4-9 and 4-10 illustrate the same two post players (O5 on the left, and O2 on the offense's right side) with the ball being reversed by the same perimeter

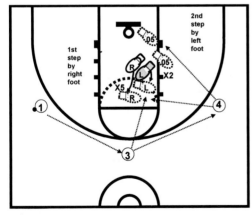

Diagram 4-9

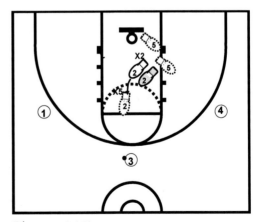

Diagram 4-10

player (01 reversing the ball to 03). The spin screen is set by 02 on X5 for 05. The defense elects to switch the spin screen to hopefully defend this action. The offense can easily counter that defensive adjustment with the actual spin screener (02, in this case) executing either a reverse pivot and sealing off X5 or a front pivot (to execute a swim move) and sealing off his new defender (X5).

Diagram 4-9 illustrates the footwork of the offense executing the (02 screening 05) spin screen being defended with a defensive switch. 02 then executes a reverse pivot to seal off his new post defender (X5). In this situation, 02 starts with his back toward the basket and breaks across the lane from the offense's right side. 02 makes a reverse pivot off his top (left) foot and then swing his lower (right) foot around to (in essence) box-out X5. With the ball centered up in 03's hands, no helpside or ballside defense is designated. X5 is even more isolated than normal, as is X2, regardless of whether X2 is attempting to defend 05 or 02.

This seal-off of his new defender puts 02 in the middle of the lane, giving 02 a higher scoring probability. Lack of height versus his new defender might not be as big of a detriment as the defender's lack of quickness when trying to match up to a (possibly) smaller but quicker offensive opponent in a high percentage scoring area. If the ball and spin screener started on the opposite of the court, the definitions of top foot, lower foot, pivot foot, and reverse pivot would be the opposite feet previously discussed.

Diagram 4-10 illustrates the same offensive (and defensive) personnel in the same locations on the court with the same type of ball reversal on the perimeter. Again, X2 switches with X5 (to help his teammate out) on the spin screen action. However, this time, 02 sets the spin screen and then makes a front crossover pivot off his top (left) foot. 02 then uses the swim technique with his contact (right) arm to seal off X5 in the same location. This technique places 02 in the same ideal location/position to be able to attack X5 in a very high percentage scoring area, but with a different type of footwork technique. Again, if on the opposite side of the court, all the footwork would be the same except with the opposite feet.

For offensive post players to be adept at scoring from the blocks, coaching staffs should teach all post players to use the necessary footwork techniques described.

Anytime an offensive post player is flashing to the ball or can catch the ball without being completely fronted by the defense, the player reaches for the pass with both hands outstretched. If the post player is in a stationary position, the post player should stagger his feet so that the contact foot (the foot closest to the post defender) is farther in front of the other foot to help seal off the defender.

Simultaneously, as the ball is being caught, the post player takes a small hop, landing on both feet at the same time, which allows the offensive player to choose either foot as the pivot foot and, therefore, the opposite foot as the free foot. The post player chins the ball to protect the ball from defenders reaching and deflecting the ball away. The post player's elbows should be sticking out to keep the defenders farther away. The post player looks over his high shoulder to read the individual post defender and to search for any possible collapsing double-down defenders from the defensive perimeter. The post player does not want to use the dribble unless he is advancing the ball to the basket and only then after he has made the appropriate reads and searches.

Show-and-Go-Opposite Drop-Step Post Move

The first post move is commonly called the show-and-go-opposite drop-step move. This scoring move is for stationary post players as well as for post players who have flashed to the ball (by the many different means previously discussed.)

The post player makes the small two-step hop *as* he catches the pass, chins the ball, and snaps his head to look over the top shoulder. The small, two-step hop will have both of the post player's feet land back on the floor simultaneously, giving the post player the freedom of having either foot as his new pivot foot and, likewise, the opposite foot as the free foot. Quickly looking over the top shoulder will allow the post player with the ball to see any defensive perimeter players who are attempting to double-down on him from above. At the same time, either seeing or not seeing his own post defender's position allows the offensive post player to act accordingly.

Quickly seeing the double-down defenders allows the post player to kick the ball back out on the perimeter to the open teammate for a probable open shot. If the ball is kicked out to perimeter players and they then score from the outside, the double-downs from the defensive team will most likely decrease. This defensive adjustment will give the offensive post players more opportunities to attack the defense in a more isolated manner. This adjustment greatly increases an offensive post player's chances of scoring from the inside against a solo defender.

If the post player looks over the top shoulder to search for double-down defenders, he should also be able to read his defensive opponent at the same time if he has not already determined his counterpart's location and position. When looking over the top shoulder, he will also see if his post defender is playing on the high side or he will not likely see him if the defender is playing him on the low (baseline) side. If the offensive player looks over his shoulder and sees nothing, he should show and go opposite toward the middle, which means that he should show the ball low and drop-step toward the middle with his higher foot being the free foot that is drop-stepping into the lane.

Diagram 4-11 illustrates a show-and-go-opposite drop-step move, starting from the same side of the lane and with X4 playing 04 on the baseline or low side, which means that 04's contact side is on the baseline (low) side. With the contact side being the opposite side as previously discussed, 04's pivot foot, his free foot, and his show shoulder are all the opposite as previously discussed. In this case, 04's contact side would be his left side, meaning he would raise the ball toward his left shoulder and drop-step toward the middle, with his free foot being the left foot while his left foot is the pivot foot.

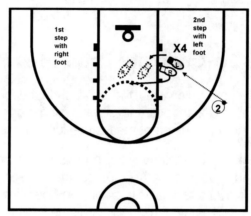

Diagram 4-11

After making his drop-step, 04 would have to continue in the same direction to shoot a left-handed lay-up or baby hook shot (in this case), or 04 could make a front pivot off his inside foot (in this case, it would be the right foot) to square up to face the basket for a turn-around jump shot. With his back to the basket, the inside foot would be his right foot, and he would have to square up to the basket by swinging his left foot around, or 04 could fake the jump shot and use an up-and-under move, still making the right foot his final pivot foot before actually shooting the ball (Diagram 4-12).

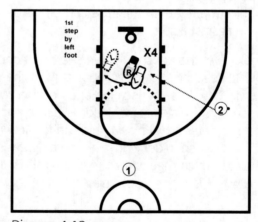

Diagram 4-12

Diagram 4-13 shows (04) looking over his top shoulder and upon seeing the post defender (X4), 04 realizes the post defender is shading toward his high side. Therefore, 04 should make the same show-and-go-opposite drop-step move, but should use the baseline foot as the free foot to use for the drop-step to the basket. As 04 makes his drop-step move, he should give the post defender a slight vision of the basketball by showing the ball over his right shoulder before actually drop-stepping in the opposite direction toward the baseline.

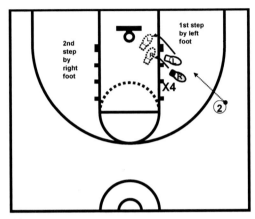

Diagram 4-13

The teaching point of emphasis phrase coaching staffs should constantly use is *Show and go opposite*. The actual showing of the ball should be done with both hands still chinning the ball in a strong manner, held closely to the chest. 04 should slightly raise the ball just above shoulder height to allow the post defender to see the ball and, therefore, use the ball as bait. 04 could also use his right shoulder as a slight fake. 04 must not allow the defender to be able to grab or to deflect the ball, when he shows the ball to lure the defender to lean toward the direction opposite of where he actually wants to take the ball.

04 makes a reverse pivot with his top foot being the pivot foot and his lower foot being the free foot that swings and drop-steps. When the post player uses the drop-step move toward the baseline (with the top foot as the pivot foot), the post player begins by lining up on the notch above the block. This location gives the post player the best angles for successful power moves to the basket.

When the actual drop-step is made, a low and hard power dribble should be made to advance the ball even closer to the basket. The post player should have been able to seal off his defender with the drop-step, and he should sit down on the thigh of the post defender to further seal his defender off. Before the post player picks up his pivot foot (the right foot, in this situation), he must make a power dribble by slamming the ball down hard with both hands between both feet. After slamming the ball down, while the ball is still in the air, the offensive post player should take a quick chicken step, while advancing the ball and his location toward the basket. When he lands from the quick chicken step, he again makes a two-foot jump stop, giving the post player the luxury of again choosing which foot will be the free foot and which foot is the pivot foot.

At the end of 04's chicken step, and aggressive power dribble, he takes his power shot high and soft off the glass. The power shot off the drop-step is probably the only shot in basketball that should not be taken with the shoulders square-up to the basket. If the shooter defeats his original defender and then squares up to take the shot, a second defender could rotate over to block the shot. The power shot should be taken with the feet at a 45-degree angle toward the basket to protect both the ball and the actual shot from helpside defenders, who are rotating over to help.

If the offensive post player were on the offense's left side of the lane to post up and attack, the same show, go opposite and drop-step moves toward the baseline or toward the middle could obviously be executed with the same footwork; but with opposite feet acting as the pivot and free feet.

The Olajuwon Whirl Move

The initial location of the post player should always be the same, regardless of whether the post player has decided which post move he will actually use. Again, the ideal position/location of the post player is the notch above the block. This position gives the offensive post player much better angles whether the post player attacks the defender and the basket on the baseline side or attacks the defense toward the middle of the lane.

As with the drop-step move, the post player should make the same small hop and land on both feet at the same time as he receives the inside pass. Again, either foot could be chosen to be the free foot and the pivot foot, which permits the post player to be able to attack either the baseline or the middle of the court. To prevent a traveling call, his two-foot hop must happen at the same instant the post player actually catches the ball.

The search for collapsing double-down defenders as well as the reading of the individual post defender is exactly the same as previously described—that is, chinning the ball before snapping the head and looking over the high shoulder. Once the read of the post defender and the search for the collapsing defenders is made by the offensive post player, the post player should show the ball and go in the opposite direction. But in this situation, the post player uses the contact foot (the foot nearest the defense) to make a front pivot that is actually away from the defense (since the offensive player's back is toward the defense).

Diagram 4-14 demonstrates an example of the post player catching the ball on the right side of the lane. After making his read and search and finding that the post defender is shading him on the high side, this time the offensive post player uses the (right) contact foot as the free foot and makes a 180-degree front pivot away from the defender (toward the baseline). It is imperative that the post player steps with that free right foot toward the basket—not laterally away from the defender. Just as in the perimeter attack of a lone defender or the inside attack of the lone defender, the offensive driver uses his own body to screen and/or seal off his defender, but in the drop-step method, the actual sealing off of the defender is with the backside, the back, and the legs. With the Olajuwon move (named for Hakeem Olajuwon), the sealing off of the post defender is done with the chest and side after the offensive post player has already pivoted and is facing the basket. Sealing off the defender in this manner denies the defender any space needed to help provide a good angle of pursuit to cut the offensive post player off on his power move to the basket.

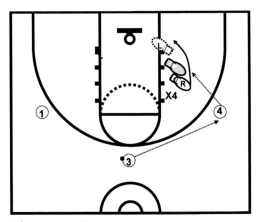

Diagram 4-14

Before the post player actually lifts up his (left) pivot foot, the ball must be dribbled with a low and hard dribble, advancing toward the basket with the first dribble landing just to the outside of the free foot. Once the first dribble is used, the post player must determine whether to continue dribbling or to kill the dribble. If the dribble is to be killed, another little bunny hop should take place and both feet should land simultaneously. This move allows the offensive post player the opportunity to use either foot as the new pivot foot.

After the advancing dribble has been killed and the two-foot bunny hop has been executed, the feet should again be at a 45-degree angle toward the basket—not squaring up to the basket as most shooters should do on the perimeter. O4 has already freed himself from X4 with the Olajuwon whirl move, but O4 must be cognizant of the fact that good defenses will have a rotating helpside defender rotating over to also attempt to stop the inside scoring of O4. Being at a 45-degree angle allows O4 to protect the ball from the next defender as well as to give himself a good opportunity to score on any and all defenders (Diagram 4-15). This move is the only time that any shooter should ever not be square-up to the basket.

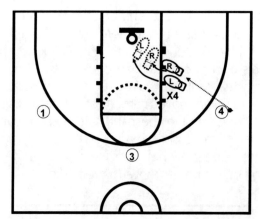

Diagram 4-15

Diagram 4-16 shows an example of the offensive post player (04) chinning the ball, as he makes the small, two-foot hop and immediately searching and reading the defense to find X4 (this time) on the low side. This example demonstrates that 04 has read the defense and decided to use the Olajuwon whirl move to attack and defeat X4 toward the middle of the lane. 04 swings the free foot (the baseline foot, which is the left foot on this side of the lane) completely around toward the middle of the lane and the basket with a front pivot off the right pivot foot (shaded foot in Diagram 4-16.). A lay-up, baby hook, or a turn-around jump shot (using a front pivot off the right heel) would finish the offensive action in the middle of the free throw lane.

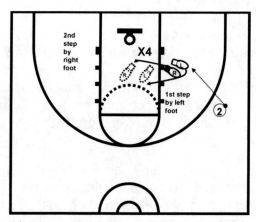

Diagram 4-16

Diagram 4-17 demonstrates another pivoting technique any post player should use once arriving to the middle of the free throw lane. Post players use this pivot after using either a show-and-go-opposite drop-step move or an Olajuwon whirl move. This post move frees 04 from X4 and places him in the middle of the lane with the basketball. Similar to a perimeter player who dribble drives and penetrates to the basket for a jump shot, post players also could use the same footwork to square up to the basket for a jump shot. In this case, if 04 is going to take a jump shot after driving to the left, he would front pivot off the inside (right) heel and swing the left foot around to square up to the basket for the short jump shot.

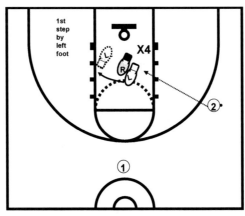
Diagram 4-17

Front Outside Pivot (and Square-Up) Move

Once again, as the pass is made to the post player (05, in this example), the post player should simultaneously make the small, two-foot hop and snap his head and look over the top shoulder—the high shoulder away from the basket. This post move is not the (Jack) Sikma inside pivot (and square-up) move that will be described later, but can be utilized in the same manner.

Both of these post moves are primarily used by post players who cannot read the lone post defender's position (X5, in this case). The post defender is not half or three-quarter fronting the offense (on either side: high or low) or may not be making physical contact with the offensive post player in any manner. This type of defensive positioning prevents the offensive post player from seeing or feeling the defender. The post player must pivot and square up to face the basket and also to find his defender. Facing the basket allows the post player to see the basket as well as to locate the defense by sight instead of by feel. To square up to the basket, the post player could utilize either foot as the pivot foot and the opposite foot as the free foot.

The only difference between the front outside pivot (and square-up) move and the Sikma move is the direction of the initial pivot. Using the front outside pivot (and square-up) move, the post player could make a front pivot—that is actually away from the basket as well as the defender, since the defender is between the basket and the offensive player with the ball—with either foot as the pivot foot and swing the (opposite) free foot 180 degrees back toward the basket without using the dribble. This pivot accomplishes the goal of the offensive post player being in a square-up position directly facing the post defender as well as the basket.

Since the dribble has not been used but the pivot foot has been established, 05 can use the appropriate move that is dependent upon the way the defense is playing the post player, just as an offensive perimeter would do.

After facing up to the basket, if X5 is playing up tight on 05, 05 could use the front crossover pivot or the blast move. These moves are the same moves that are taught to every perimeter player (as well as every post player). The front crossover pivot is going in the opposite direction of the chosen pivot foot, and the blast move is going in the same direction of the actual pivot foot. If the defender is playing softly on the post player, the post player could decide to rise up and take a jump shot without having to utilize the dribble or could use the dribble to advance the ball to the basket.

Diagram 4-18 illustrates offensive post player 05 (with his back to the basket and to X5) on the offense's left side of the court using the right foot (shaded foot in Diagram 4-18) as the pivot foot. 05 makes a front pivot (actually away from the basket) and the defender toward the baseline by swinging the (free) left foot around the right pivot foot.

Diagram 4-19 shows the same post player with his back toward the basket and defender on the offense's left side of the court. The post player makes a front pivot away from the basket and the defender, but turns toward the middle of the free throw lane by using the left foot as the pivot foot and stepping toward the middle with his right free foot.

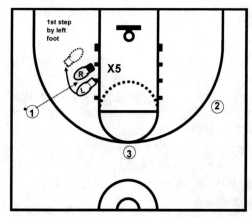

Diagram 4-18

Diagram 4-19

The Sikma Inside Pivot (and Square-Up) Move

The Sikma inside pivot move obviously got its name from the outstanding post player (Jack Sikma), who played college basketball at Illinois Wesleyan University for Coach Dennis Bridges, started his NBA career with the Seattle Supersonics, and basically created the specific footwork in this offensive post move. As mentioned earlier, this offensive technique and post move is not the same, but it can be used in the same manner as the front outside pivot (and square-up) move previously described.

The only difference between these two offensive post moves is the direction of the initial pivot. The Sikma inside pivot move has the free foot stepping toward the basket and the defender in a 180-degree reverse pivot. This move also puts the offensive post player in a square-up position, facing both the basket as well as the defender, but it also creates space for the post player as he actually reverse pivots toward the post defender. This move is also used by perimeter players to create separation between the ball handler and the ball defender.

Diagram 4-20 illustrates a Sikma move with the ball being caught by the post player on the offense's left side of the lane. After the quick two-foot hop, the chinning of the ball with both elbows extended, and the read and search, the post player (04, in this case) decides to use the top (left) foot as the pivot foot. This move allows him to use the right foot as the free foot as he makes a 180-degree reverse pivot. With the post player's back originally toward the basket, a reverse pivot is actually swinging the free foot toward the basket and also toward the defender. This technique places the post player in a square-up position, facing the basket and the defender, with the left foot (which now the baseline foot) being the pivot foot. At this point, 04 can attack X4 in the same variety of ways previously described.

Diagram 4-20

The Sikma move is a post player's pivot that could be called or described either as a reverse pivot toward the basket or an inside pivot. Diagram 4-21 illustrates the same Sikma move with the ball being caught by the post player with his back to the basket on the same left side of the lane. But in this scenario, the post player decides to use the lower (right) foot as the pivot foot, which makes the free foot the left foot. The left foot makes a 180-degree reverse pivot toward the basket and the post defender, putting the post player square-up to the basket, with the new lower foot (toward the baseline) being the left foot and also the free foot. The only problem with this approach could be that 04 might end up squaring up to the basket, but below the block. This position could take away some of the ideal shooting and driving angles because of 04's vertical depth in relation to the free throw lane and low-post block. If that is the case and that is a move 04 wants to use with a great deal of frequency, he simply must start his initial post-up position higher up the free throw lane line.

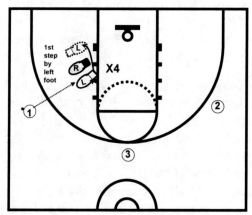

Diagram 4-21

The Sikma moves could obviously be used on both sides of the court with either the right foot or the left foot being the initial pivot foot. In these two illustrations, the right foot was first used as a pivot foot, and afterwards, the left foot was used as a pivot foot. On the right offensive side of the court, the opposite foot would be used as the pivot foot.

Summary

Many breakdown drills can be created and used to work on the various offensive post play techniques previously described. A few of the techniques that should be taught and then continually repetitioned in breakdown drills include:
- Getting open to catch the ball
- The techniques of actually catching the various types of inside passes
- The various post moves (after the catch) that should be used versus the various ways that post defenses can be played
- The actual shooting the ball off the different offensive post moves

The more a coaching staff can develop drills that are game-realistic and can integrate the use of several different techniques at the same time, the more productive and time-efficient those drills will be. The drills are learning stations for the players, teaching and demonstration stations for the coaching staff, and then should become observation, evaluation, and corrective criticism stations for the staff and the players. Coaches should always keep the drills game-realistic, competitive, and intense.

Keeping the drills short, but repetitive, seems to make the drills more productive. Many drills can be created to fit the coaching staff's personality, the players' needs, and the circumstances that the team is in. Several shooting drills—such as the dot shots drill as well as many others—are thoroughly described in the section of Chapter 1 that describes the fundamentals and stretching daily stations routine.

As important of a concept as offensive post play is to the overall offensive schemes of a basketball team, the art of pivoting is an integral part of the actual post play game, which makes the art of pivoting essential to the offensive success of a basketball team.

5

Important Pivots
of the Rebounder

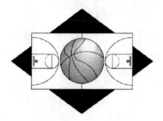

*"You can dribble too much and you can shoot
too much, but you cannot rebound too much."*
—Anonymous

A team must be able to score and also play defense in order to win games. For a team to be able to score, that team must have possession of the basketball. Possession of the ball always gives a team a chance of scoring; while maintaining possession of the ball, the opponent has absolutely no chance of scoring. Possession of the basketball is, therefore, of vital importance to the success of a basketball team.

It is extremely important to use all methods of gaining and maintaining possession of the basketball. One very important way of acquiring possession of the ball is by forcing the opponent to commit turnovers. A negative way of getting possession of the ball is after the opposition has scored and the ball is to be taken out-of-bounds by the scored-upon defensive team. Possibly the most important way of getting possession or maintaining possession of the basketball is by the rebound from any type of missed shot—whether the rebound is an offensive rebound or a defensive rebound.

Maintaining possession of the basketball via offensive rebounding is very important. Shooters who miss shots and see the opposition rebound the majority of their missed shots may cause those shooters to become very hesitant to shoot the ball. When an offensive team is hesitant about shooting the ball, the overall offensive production will most likely decrease. Decreases in offense most likely will mean decreases in the W column.

In addition, getting offensive rebounds gives the offensive team excellent opportunities for second shots. These second shots, or what are called stickbacks, are probably the most ideal shots that an offensive team can have.

A planned offensive play or entry most likely cannot match the shot opportunities that stickbacks can give to an offense. An offensive team that excels at offensive rebounding also relieves a great deal of pressure on its shooters, because those shooters realize that their missed shot does not necessarily mean a change in possession of the basketball. More than likely, relieving pressure on shooters improves shooters' performances and effectiveness. Even if an offensive player gets the offensive rebound, shoots, and misses, absolutely no organization is made on the part of the opposition's defense to attempt another defensive box-out on the second shot by the offense.

With both the defensive and the offensive teams understanding the importance of rebounding the basketball, defensive teams will value the defensive rebound, while offensive teams will also place a high premium on offensive rebounds. The most important (as well as the most common) factor in a team trying to get defensive rebounds and also preventing offensive rebounds is the defensive box-out by the defender on the (potential) offensive rebounder.

In a short summary, the importance of possessions is so great that it puts a tremendous value on defensive and offensive rebounds. The significance of successful execution of defensive box-outs and beating the opponents' defensive box-outs (for offensive rebounds) cannot be overstated. Defensive rebounders must understand the importance and must be able to execute the defensive box-out. Offensive rebounders should comprehend and believe in the value of the offensive counter to a defensive box-out.

In the execution of the defensive box-out, proper footwork, using both the front and reverse pivots, is the first and the most important component needed for successful box-outs. Both the front and the reverse pivots are required in certain situations when executing defensive box-outs.

The front and reverse pivots are two methods of just starting the actual defensive box-out. The pivots are only the initial phase of the box-out. The making contact with the opposition while searching for the missed shot is also of great importance, but that component comes after the successful pivots by the defender to make contact with the offensive opponent.

Once the contact is made by the defender with the potential offensive rebounder, the remaining basic fundamentals of boxing out are all the same. After the initial phase of making contact with the opposition is done, the defensive player should have a wide base, with his elbows held at shoulder height, extended, bent at 90-degree angles, and pulled backward. The elbows are up and held back to form a V. That V is used to somewhat hold the offensive rebounder so that he can be controlled by the defender.

The head of the defender is up to be able to see where the ball is coming off the backboard. The hands of the defender should remain up to first keep the defender from the temptation of reaching down to hold the opponent as well as to also be able to grab the (defensive) rebound.

Short, choppy steps are to be used to stay in front of the offensive opponent, who is trying to avoid the defender and get around him to retrieve the rebound. These short, choppy steps are used to maintain balance and possess a quickness of the defender to cut off the paths of the opponent to the missed shot.

Box-out defenders must keep their hands off the opponent for two main reasons: to prevent defensive holding fouls and also to give the defender a chance to grab the missed shot. If his hands are down, how is he to grab the rebound? If the offensive rebounder is much stronger physically, the defender should stagger the feet to offer more resistance to prevent the offensive opponent from pushing the defender underneath the basket, where there are no defensive rebounds.

The phrases used to teach and reinforce the boxing out technique are:
• Pivot and make contact.
• Keep your elbows high and locked.
• Make a V with your bent elbows.
• Keep your elbows back.
• See your man with your body (not your eyes).
• Use short, choppy steps.
• Don't get shoved under the basket.
• Hands up and head up to see the ball and to get it.

These basic fundamentals are extremely important, but if the initial step of the defensive box-out is not performed correctly, the box-out can never be successful. The first phase and the most important phase of the box-out is the initial quick contact that must be made by each defender. This contact is initiated by either the front (crossover) pivot or the reverse pivot. Both pivots should be used in certain circumstances because both have specific advantages that must be utilized.

Diagram 5-1 illustrates the stances for all five defenders playing in a man-to-man defensive system. The brackets represent an individual defender's stance facing toward the right. The diagram shows the left arm, the right arm and the player's back of all five

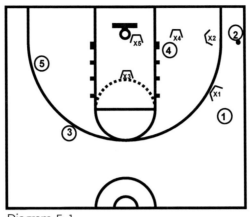

Diagram 5-1

defenders. This diagram shows X2 defending 02 with the ball. X1 is in the defensive position that is one pass away, with X4 being the ballside post defender. X5 and X3 are both helpside defenders more than one perimeter pass away from the basketball.

Boxing Out the Shooter

Defenders should only use the front pivot when defensively boxing out an opposing shooter, while all off-the-ball defenders should use the reverse pivot to make the initial contact with their offensive opponent. On-the-ball defenders want to put as much pressure on the shooter as possible. Such pressure comes from being as close to the shooter as possible, having a hand up. Defenders should not try to *block* every shot by the opposition, but they should attempt to *alter* every shot the opponents take. A phrase used to help reinforce this philosophy is telling defenders: "Don't leave the ground (to block the shot) until the shooter leaves the ground."

As the shot is taken, the defender on the shooter should be facing the shooter with his hand up high near the actual shooting hand of the shooter. The defender's momentum should be going slightly forward. The defender continues that momentum and makes the front (crossover) pivot to initiate the contact as soon as he reads the direction that the shooter is going to take toward the missed shot. The front pivot allows the defender to quickly make contact with the opponent, as well as to pick up both the sight of the ball and where the ball is going to ricochet.

Conversely, for the shooter to rebound, he must see the ball and react to it. Since the defender initially is facing the shooter, he cannot see both the ball and rim immediately after the ball is shot. Therefore, the defender should first respond to the offensive player's reaction to the missed shot and then, as quickly as possible, look for the ball. The front pivot allows the defender to immediately gain vision of the ball and start to read the direction that the ball will take after hitting the backboard and/or rim.

The defender front crossover pivots directly into the path the shooter (now the offensive rebounder) takes to go after the missed shot. If the shooter follows his shot and goes to his left, the defender front (crossover) pivot by stepping across with his left foot (and pivot off of his right foot) directly into the path of the rebounder. If the shooter follows his shot and cuts to his right, the defender should then make the same front crossover pivot, but step across with his right foot. The defender can even slide a step with the shooter before performing the front pivot to make the initial contact.

Defensively, Diagram 5-2 is an example of the correct technique and footwork for the defensive box-out on a shooter (02) that goes to his left for the offensive rebound. If the shooter follows the shot by going to his right, the defender front pivots by stepping forward with the right foot across the offensive player's path.

Diagram 5-2

On the offensive side of the ball concerning the footwork for offensive rebounds, Diagram 5-3 shows the proper footwork when the shooter cuts to his right to attempt to offensive rebound the shot. Coaches could use a phrase that clearly explains to the on-the-ball defender how to perform the correct front (crossover) pivot box-out

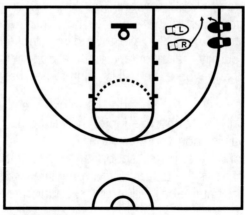

Diagram 5-3

technique: When the shooter steps to go for the rebound, the defender should make a front crossover pivot and step into his opponent's path with the hands up as if the defender were going to punch the opponent in the jaw. While not wanting the defender to actually punch the opponent, this phrase stresses to the defender to be the aggressor and to quickly step into the path of the offensive opponent, as well as to hold the elbows high. Coaching points of emphasis and phrases that coaches can use to stress the proper techniques once the initial contact is made with the hips, legs, and butt include:

- Go butt to gut.
- Maintain the contact with short, choppy steps.
- Keep the hands up.
- Keep the elbows high and locked.
- Go get it.

Boxing Out One Pass Away

All off-the-ball and one-pass-away defenders should utilize the reverse pivot to initiate contact with the opposition's offensive rebounder. These defenders include most ballside post defenders who are in a half or three-quarter front position. In a man-to-man defense, all one-pass-away defenders would be in a denial stance. This stance is very conducive for them to easily reverse pivot off of the trail foot and swing the lead foot around quickly into the path of where the offensive opponent is basically being forced to go.

The initial denial (of the pass) stance prevents the opponent from going in that direction, so his only choice would be to try to go around the defender. The reverse pivot makes it easy for the defender to initiate the contact of the box-out and also quickly pick up the flight of the shot so he can track down the defensive rebound.

The defenders initiate the contact with the opponent on the box-out. Reverse pivoting allows the defender to quickly find the ball and estimate where the ricochet will occur. The reverse pivot is the only method to accomplish both goals.

Diagram 5-4 illustrates the reverse pivots made by different man-to-man defensive players who are one pass away from the shooter. In Diagram 5-4, 04 has the ball in the deep corner. X1 is denying the pass from 04 to 01 near the free throw line extended. X5 is denying the inside pass to 05, who is posting up at the ballside block. X3 and X2 are playing helpside defense on their respective men, who are two perimeter passes away from the ball.

X4 makes a front pivot to follow the rule of using the front pivot to box out a shooter. X5 and X1 both make reverse pivots by swinging their free foot 180 degrees around into the expected (and only) path that the offensive opponents have to go to the basket.

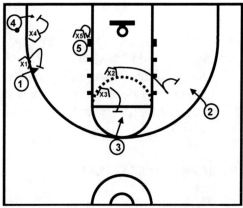

Diagram 5-4

The top foot is always the free foot, and the pivot foot is always the lower foot. X1 and X5 both swing the right foot around to make a reverse pivot off of the left foot to initiate contact on their defensive box-out assignment. X3 and X2's techniques of boxing out will be discussed in the next section.

Boxing Out More Than One Pass Away

For all man-to-man defensive players that are off-the-ball and more than one pass away, their initial position should be sagging off their actual offensive man either one step manside or one step ballside. Their location/position should be in a ball-you-man flat triangle one to one-and-a-half steps off of the passing line, and their stance should be in a pistols stance with their head on a swivel, seeing the ball and seeing their man. These defenders are known as help side defenders.

When the ball is shot, the helpside defenders sprint under control at their man and shade and run at the high shoulder of their opponent. This move is similar to the fanning overplay of the on-the-ball defenders when playing the man-to-man defense. The fanning influence that the helpside defenders are making should force the offensive players to make the predictable cut more toward the baseline (away from the defender).

When fanning the weakside offensive rebounding opponent, that offensive opponent will want to avoid the box-out, so he most likely will run in the perceived open channel toward the basket and the ball and, therefore, runs to the outside of the defender. When the defender gets close enough to his man on his approach, the defender makes a reverse pivot into the outside path of the opponent. Since the defense overplays the opposition's offensive rebounders with the fanning style of play, it makes the opposition much more predictable as to what direction he is going to use to approach the basket. Therefore, the defensive rebounder can very well safely predict the direction his offensive opponent will cut for the offensive rebound. It is much easier for that helpside defender to then be able to make the reverse pivot and successfully box out the opposition's rebounder.

The defender should always initiate the contact with the opponent *outside* of the free throw lane. If contact is made in the lane itself, often times the defender is boxed in (instead of the defender boxing out the opponent) as the missed shot bounces over the defenders' heads, giving that weakside offensive opponent a much greater chance of getting the offensive rebound and maintaining possession of the ball.

Diagram 5-5 illustrates a shot from the deep corner on the right side of the court. In this illustration, X1 defends 01, who is the shooter from the deep corner on the right side of the floor. X2 is denying the up pass to 02 at the free throw line extended and is in a one pass away defensive position. X2 would be in a denial stance with his left foot being up and he would reverse pivot off of his lower (right) foot and lead with his left foot as he makes butt-to-gut contact with his opponent (02). X5 is more than one perimeter pass from the ball, sagging off and guarding 05, while settling in at the top of the key. X3 is sagging off and setting up defensively in the middle of the free throw lane. X3 is guarding 03, who is three perimeter passes from the ball. X4 is also playing helpside defense in the lane, while defending 04 in the weakside block area. 04 is defined as being more than one perimeter pass from the ball, unless 04 would flash to the ballside post area (high or low), where he would become a player one pass away from the ball.

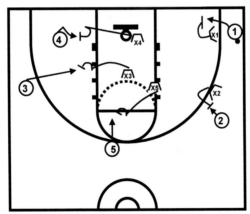

Diagram 5-5

If 01 cannot pass the ball to a teammate and is influenced to shoot the ball from the deep corner, X4 would quickly go across the lane to headhunt the high (inside) shoulder of 04 (in this case, the right shoulder) to initiate the contact outside of the free throw lane. This should influence 04 to predictably go toward the baseline, which is where you want him to go. X4 would reverse pivot into 04 by swinging the top foot (left, in this case) and pivot off of the bottom or the baseline foot (right) and make contact (ideally, outside of the lane) to box out his opponent (04).

X3 would follow the same techniques by fanning the opponent and also use the right (the lower or baseline) foot as the pivot foot to reverse pivot into 03 (hopefully, outside of the free throw lane.)

X5 would also try to influence 05 into a predictable path to the basket and likewise would reverse pivot off the right foot, while swinging the left foot directly into 05's supposedly open path to the rebound.

Diagram 5-6 illustrates the team concept of all five defensive players executing the appropriate techniques of boxing out from their specific situation. X2 uses the correct front pivot technique to box out the shooter (02).

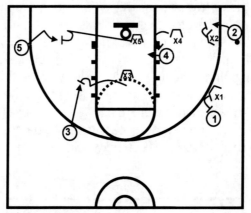

Diagram 5-6

X4 is a ballside post defender who is one pass away and makes a reverse pivot off of the lower (right) foot so that he can swing his left foot around to make the same butt-to-gut contact into 04. X1 is also one pass away on the perimeter, and he should make the same reverse pivot off of the same lower (right) foot. Both X4 and X1 then swing the left free foot into the predictable path of their offensive opponent to initially establish contact with their respective opponents. They then must maintain that contact and stay between their man and the ball.

X3, as a helpside defender who is two perimeter passes away from the ball, reacts to the shot, and should quickly go across the lane to search out his opponent to box out. X3 should influence 03 to go toward the baseline by running at his higher (right) shoulder and should try to make contact with his opponent outside of the lane. X3 makes a reverse pivot off the lower (right) foot and swings the left foot into 03's predictable path to the basket. X5 is also a helpside defender, and he, too, goes across the lane, fanning 05 toward the baseline. X5 also makes a reverse pivot off of the low (right) foot by swinging his left foot into 05 either outside of the lane or as close to the edge of the free throw lane as possible. X3 and X5 are strongly urged to make the initial contact outside of the free throw lane to prevent getting boxed in and giving their respective opponents a greater advantage for the offensive rebound.

You cannot have one weak link in a defensive team's box-out effort, or the opposition will start getting more and more offensive rebounds. Surrendering offensive rebounds truly demoralizes a defensive team that works hard on both on-the-ball and off-the-ball defense, forces the opposition to miss shots, and then gives up even closer shots to the basket on the opponent's offensive stickbacks.

If a defensive team can minimize the opponent's number of offensive possessions and shots, that defensive team has a much greater chance of winning the game. Defensive rebounds not only limit the number of possessions and shots by the opposition, but also maximize the number of possessions the defensive-turned-offensive team has to score. Without the defensive box-out, minimal defensive rebounds will be available for the defensive team and a maximum number of opponent's offensive rebounds. Without the proper box-out techniques, minimal defensive rebounds will occur. Proper footwork and pivoting are two of the most important defensive rebounding and box-out techniques.

The Defensive Rebound and the Outlet Pass

Besides eliminating the opponent's offensive team their possession of the basketball, another important factor is the defensive team then quickly converting from defense to offense. An integral part of the defensive rebound is the outlet pass after the defensive box-out has successfully been executed and the defensive rebound has been claimed. A defensive team does not want to expend large amounts of effort on the defensive side of the ball, make the proper defensive box-out techniques, secure the defensive rebound, and then give the opposition the ball back because of poor outlet passing techniques.

Grabbing the defensive rebound concludes the opposition's possession of the basketball. It also begins the actual possession of the ball for the defensive rebounding team. This approach obviously halts the scoring chances of the opposition and begins the scoring opportunities of the initial defensive team.

After the defense has successfully boxed out the offensive opponent and grabbed the defensive rebound, the rebounder must make an outlet pass to initiate a fast break. If the fast break style is not utilized by that team, the outlet pass must still be used to get the ball into a more capable ball handler's hands to bring the ball down the court successfully, regardless of the speed the (new) offensive team elects to utilize. To do so effectively, the defensive rebounder that obtains the rebound must make a front pivot (away from the opposition's resistance) before the actual outlet pass can be made.

Diagram 5-7 shows a defensive rebounder gaining possession of the rebound on the original defense's left side of the court. The rebounder should chin the ball (as offensive post players are taught to do when catching the inside pass), front pivot (that is actually away from the new defensive pressure) off the outside foot (in this case,

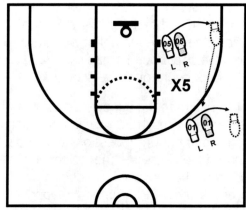

Diagram 5-7

the right foot), and swing the inside foot (left) to turn away from potential opposing defenders. This pivot allows the rebounder to face all outlet receivers as well as his basket, before making the pass to his teammate (01).

The receiver catching the outlet pass (01) must get open so that he can be an open pass receiver. Proper footwork possibly by making V-cuts to free himself from an opponent very likely will be necessary to get open so that the ball can be placed in a better ball handler's hands to speed up a possible fast break. Once he is open, he must meet the pass before catching the ball. Upon meeting the outlet pass from 05, 01 should also make a front pivot (away from the initial defender) toward the sideline (away from all other defenders located in the middle of the court). This move should be done by front pivoting off of the outside foot (also the right foot in this case) and swinging the inside (left) foot toward the sideline. He should also chin the ball and immediately look to advance the ball down the court in the quickest and most secure method, via dribble or passing ahead to an open teammate. This technique allows 01 to protect the ball before knowing how much defensive pressure he will immediately receive. This front pivot also gives him the full view of the frontcourt as well as his teammates. This front pivot is the safest as well as a very safe method. Some coaches believe that the reverse pivot should be used at this point, as it may be a little quicker. However, safety is preferable over the possibly minute increase in speed of the reverse pivot versus the front pivot by the outlet pass receiver.

On the opposite side of the court, Diagram 5-8 shows a defensive rebounder who has made the defensive box-out and grabbed the defensive rebound. This rebounder (04) will also chin the ball and turn away from the middle where most opposing defenders should be located. This move is done by front pivoting (away from the defensive pressure) off of the outside pivot foot (left, in this case) and swinging the free inside foot (right) again toward the sideline.

This outlet pass is made to the guard (02) who also front pivots off of the outside pivot foot (left) and swings the inside free foot (right) toward the outside (away from

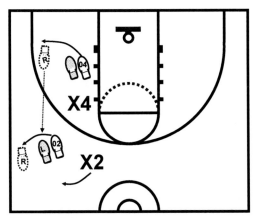

Diagram 5-8

most defenders). This front pivot by both the defensive rebounder/outlet passer and the pass receiver again allows both (now) offensive players to protect the basketball without seeing or knowing the degree of pressure they will face upon possession of the basketball. Once they have faced and then gauged the degree of the defensive pressure, they then can safely look downcourt to their own offensive basket, to also look for teammates and to advance the ball down the court via passing or dribbling.

As important of a concept as defending the ball is to the overall defensive schemes and how important defensive box-outs and outlet passes off the defensive rebound are, the art of pivoting is a vital part of all three parts of the defense. As a result, the ability to pivot is very important to the defensive and the transition success of a basketball team.

Offensive Rebounding

While the previous discussion explains how important defensive boxing out and defensive rebounding are to a defensive team, beating the opposition's defensive box-out techniques to gain offensive rebounds is equally important to offensive teams. A successful basketball team must have skills in both defensive and offensive rebounding.

The next discussion is about the appropriate techniques that should be used to overcome a good opponent's defensive box-outs. These techniques must be demonstrated, taught, and practiced as offensive players because offensive rebounding is also an important part of a team's offense.

Before the first technique is ever shown, the coaching staff should sell the team on the importance of offensive rebounds and explain how stickbacks can be a very effective way of scoring. Stickbacks can be very close to the basket and will be taken against an opponent's defense that probably will never be in more of a disorganized state than they are immediately after the offense has shot the basketball. The attitude that a coaching staff should instill in its players is to look at every missed shot by themselves or a teammate as a pass to them.

If the opposition is playing any type of a zone defense or trapping defense, it must be impressed upon the offensive team that they have a greater advantage of offensive rebounds. Because of the makeup of zone and trapping defenses, rebounding assignments are nonexistent. This disadvantage of the opposition's defense must be taken advantage of by the offense with an aggressive and positive attitude of the offense.

Three Methods of Offensive Rebounding

Three different methods can be taught to offensive rebounders on trying to defeat defensive box-outs. All three methods are somewhat different, but all three methods require pivots.

The first method is explained in this simple manner. Coaches could tell the offensive player to go butt-to-butt (with his defensive counterpart) and spin off. The offensive rebounder should see the ball being shot, make a quick reverse pivot, and make contact with the defender to literally spin off of him. Either foot could be used as the pivot foot to make the reverse pivot.

The second method requires the use of a front crossover pivot and the swim technique. Using the swim move with the arm closest to the defender should be stressed.

It is best to use the left foot as the pivot foot (and, therefore, the right foot as the free foot) to make a front crossover step when attacking the defender's right side. If the offensive rebounder wants to go to his own right side, it is best to use the left foot as the free (front crossover) foot and make the right foot the pivot foot.

The third method is for the offensive player to step backward and break physical contact with the defensive player. When the defensive opponent looks over his shoulder to find the offensive player, the offensive player makes a front crossover pivot and attacks the shoulder opposite the one the defender turned to search for him.

Circle Box-Out Drill

One of the most productive drills utilized for the boxing out part of rebounding, both offensively as defensively, is a drill called the circle box-out drill. This drill is part of the fundamental and stretching routine that was described in Chapter 1. It is very time-efficient and productive because the offensive concepts and techniques as well as the defensive concepts and techniques can be observed, evaluated, and critiqued by the coaching staff as well as practiced by an entire squad at the same time in a relatively short amount of court space and practice time.

Two pairs of players can be placed at any of the three circles or semicircles on a main court. The center jump circle and the circles at each of the possible six free throw lines (where there are two main court baskets and four side court baskets) can be used. Those seven circles with two pairs of players allow 14 players opportunities to work on defensive boxing out and 14 other players to work on defeating the defensive boxing out. This setup makes for great competition as well as excellent opportunities for coaching staffs to evaluate and correct any mistakes made by either offensive or defensive players.

A basketball is placed in the center of each circle. The defensive players face out toward their offensive opponent. The defensive players line up in various on-the-ball and off-the-ball defensive stances at the outer edge of the circle. Offensive players line up one full step to the outside of their defender, facing their defender and the ball in the center of the circle.

One of the observing coaches yells "Shot!" and each defender practices initiating contact with his opposing practice player with the appropriate pivot and continues maintaining contact with the short, choppy steps with the elbows high and locked. Each defender utilizes the correct techniques of either boxing out the shooter, boxing out a player one pass away, or boxing out a player (across the imaginary free throw lane) from the helpside. The offensive rebounder works on defeating that defensive box-out and getting the offensive rebound.

The drill is a 1-on-1 competitive drill with both a winner and a loser. For the defensive player to win, he must keep the offensive player from touching the basketball for a predetermined time (three or four seconds is a very good time limit for coaches to use). The defender loses if he is legally pushed into the circle (and theoretically under the basket, where no defensive rebounds exist). If the offensive player in this drill can legally push and shove the defensive player to the middle of the circle toward the ball, that defensive player will allow himself to be shoved under the basket in an actual game.

Each player must practice three scenarios both defensively as well as offensively each time the circle box-out drill is used in practice. One player starts on defense for two repetitions, while his partner starts on offense. They then switch for two reps with the same scenario. Each pair of practice players then move to the second scenario for two more repetitions at both the offense as well as the defense, and finish with the third scenario and two reps on offense before two reps on defense.

The three scenarios that each player practices both offensively as well as defensively are:

- The offensive player is a shooter (and therefore the defender is an on the ball defender).

- The offensive player is one pass away.
- The offensive player is more than one perimeter pass away.

In the first scenario (Diagram 5-9), each offensive practice player pretends to shoot the ball. Every defensive player (X1 and X2) works on the appropriate techniques of defending a shooter (01 and 02) before making the appropriate pivot and then the actual defensive box-out of a shooter. Each offensive player playacts as a shooter and then becomes an offensive rebounder, practicing the correct techniques of breaking contact that the defensive player makes, while then attempting to get the pseudo-offensive rebound.

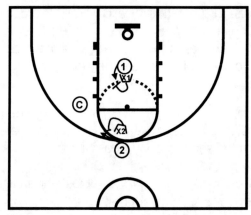

Diagram 5-9

01 breaks to his right as X1 steps across to make a front pivot with his right free foot, using the left foot as the pivot foot. With 02 breaking to his left, X2 steps across with a front pivot with his left foot as the free foot and the right foot as the pivot foot to make the box-out on 02.

After two reps, all four players switch assignments from offense to defense or defense to offense. Points are awarded to the winners of each simulated missed shot. Keeping the offensive player out of the circle and away from the ball for two or three seconds is a win for the defense. Later in the season, the time can be increased to four seconds for the defense. If an offensive player gets into the circle and touches the ball in the middle of the circle, he is declared the winner. Score is kept for each different attempt of the offensive rebounding to indicate whether it was the offensive rebounder or the defender in each pair of competitors that won the battle, with the losing players having some form of minor consequence or penalty. The offensive players should work on all of their offensive rebound moves. The staff might dictate which one they want their players to work on or it may be left up to the offensive players to choose.

As previously discussed, in the second scenario (Diagram 5-10), the offensive players pretend to be one pass away. Both defensive players (X3 and X4) work on the

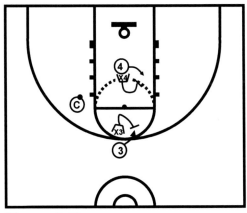

Diagram 5-10

appropriate stances and then the techniques of boxing out their specific man (03 and 04) when their man is one pass away.

When the ball is not passed, but an imaginary shot is taken by a coach or a manager, these two defenders make the appropriate pivot and then the defensive box-out. Each offensive player (03 and 04) playacts as a pass receiver and then becomes an offensive rebounder, practicing their correct techniques of avoiding the defensive box-out before then attempting to get the imaginary offensive rebound.

When the coach yells "Shot!" 03 breaks to his right as X3 (in a one-pass-away denial stance) reverse pivots off the left (lower) foot and swings his right foot into the path of 03. Meanwhile, 04 breaks to his left, so that X4 reverse pivots off the trail foot (right) and swings the free (left) foot into the path of 04 to make the initial contact of the box-out. After two reps, these players switch offensive and defensive assignments. Before starting the second pair of shots, the coach and the (imaginary) ball switch sides (of the circle) so that off-the-ball defenders practice with the ball on both sides of their offensive practice opponent.

Winners and losers are noted for each different attempt of the offensive rebounding. The offensive players should again work on one of the offensive moves they have been taught. Again, the moves they are to work on might be chosen by the coaching staff or left up to the offensive players.

The third and final scenario is illustrated in Diagram 5-11. In this scenario, the offensive player simulates being a pass receiver on the opposite side of the court from the ball. X5 plays helpside defense in the appropriate stance while guarding 05 from the opposite side of the circle (which simulates the free throw lane). The other defender (X6) plays helpside defense also in the appropriate defensive stance, while guarding 06 across the circle.

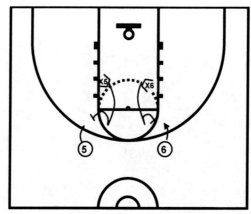

Diagram 5-11

To make this part of the drill game-realistic, all offensive players should step off the circle an extra step back from the center of the circle. The defenders want to influence their offensive opponents to go toward the outside (toward the sideline and baseline) to try to get the offensive rebound. When the coach yells "Shot," both defenders sprint across the circle (simulating the free throw lane), heading for the inside shoulder of the offensive player. When the offensive players cut toward the ball, the defensive players make a reverse pivot (off the outside foot) and swing their inside foot into the path of where they have dictated the offensive opponent to go for the rebound.

The defenders make contact with their opponents and maintain that initial contact, using the same techniques as previously discussed. If X5 approaches O5 in the proper manner, O5 is forced to his left and, therefore, cuts to his left. X5 then reverse pivots off of the right foot and swings the left foot into the path of O5 to box him out. O6 also should have been influenced by X6's approach so that he will break to his right. After his proper approach to O6, X6 then should reverse pivot off his outside foot (left) foot and should then swing his inside (the right) foot into the path of offensive player O6. Each offensive player should work on one of the offensive rebounding moves as well as first avoiding the initial contact made by the defender.

One or More Passes Away
Box-Out and Rebounding Drill

This drill features defensive box-outs as well as the counterattacks of box-outs by the offense using a larger group of offensive and defensive players. Diagram 5-12 illustrates several pairs of players in various positions and locations on the court. A coach can be the designated shooter and should move around to various locations on the floor. Each time a coach with the ball moves, it changes players from being one pass away to more than one pass away from the ball. This shift changes the initial position and stances of most defenders as well as the specific methods that those players should be

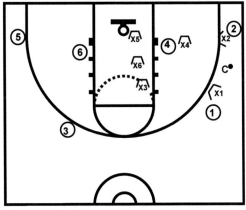

Diagram 5-12

using to make their defensive box-outs. This drill may not be as game-realistic as the subsequent drill, but its advantages are time efficiency and the concentrated amount of repetitions that take place. The drill can be shortened to observe only the stances as the ball changes locations, or it can be used to observe, evaluate, and critique all defenders' stances as well as the completed box-out and also the outlet pass.

Shell Rebounding Drill

Diagram 5-13 is a similar, but more game-realistic, drill. This drill is also set up in the (half-court) shell drill format with defensive players positioned on offensive players who are either the shooter (O2), one pass away (O1, O4, and O7), or more than one pass away (O3, O5, and O6). The drill can include perimeter players (O1, O3, and O5) as well as post players (O4, O6, and O7), and offensive players located both above (O1, O3, and O7) and below (O2, O4, O5, and O6) the free throw line extended. Every possible location and situation can and should be covered while utilizing this drill.

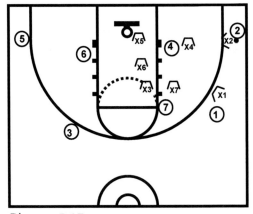

Diagram 5-13

Offensive players should change from being perimeter players to becoming inside players, and vice versa. Offensive players should switch from the right side to the left side of the floor, and vice versa. Eventually, after a designated number of repetitions, players should rotate from offense to defense, and vice versa. Defenders will not only have to drill the proper stances and locations/positions in each of their different ball-you-man flat triangles, but when the ball is finally shot, they will have to learn how to instantly select the proper techniques of boxing out both post players as well as perimeter players that are sometimes on the ballside and sometimes on the defensive helpside. Defenders will sometimes have to box out shooters as well as having to box out their opponent on both sides of the court, as well as perimeter players and also post players.

The coaching staff can limit the number of offensive players. The coaching staff can specify a certain number of passes that must take place before the designated shot (to initiate all of the action). In addition, the coaching staff can dictate the types of movement the offensive team makes before the designated shot is taken (such as off-the-ball screens, give-and-go cuts to the basket before then emptying out).

Offensive players will work on their offensive rebounding techniques and the proper footwork to defeat defensive box-outs. The coaching staff can make this drill as live as they want and as competitive as they want, with rewards and punishments to the winners and the losers.

Summary

Drills are very valuable in correcting and improving the techniques of both the offensive rebounders and the defensive rebounders. Close scrutiny and positive criticism by the coaching staff are invaluable to improving and developing players' skills and techniques in this very important, but sometimes overlooked phase of the game.

As important as rebounding is to the overall offensive and defensive schemes of a basketball team, the techniques of boxing out and/or defeating the opponents' box-out are more important. Proper pivots are integral parts of both the offensive and defensive rebounding phases of the game. Therefore, the art of pivoting is most important to the rebounding success of a basketball team.

6

Important Pivots of the Screener

*"On offense there are three unselfish team
actions that are necessary for success: passing,
screening, and moving without the ball."*
—Bill Bradley

The primary purpose for setting screens is for an offensive player to get a teammate open so that the pass receiver can free himself from his defender and then receive a pass for a high percentage shot, which can be done by using either general type of screen—the ball screen and the off-the-ball screen. In many offenses, screeners are being used more and more as potential scorers in either one of two different types of action. This first method is the original screener slipping the screen, sometimes just called slipping the screen or pick and pop. The second method is that the original screener is screened after setting the initial screen. This particular offensive action is called screen-the-screener action. Therefore, various types of screening action can now be implemented so that the actual initial screener suddenly can become the primary scorer, if not the secondary scorer.

The common factor in the action immediately after the initial screen (whether it is a ball screen or an off-the-ball screen) is some form of a pivot by that screener. This pivot by the screener is used to continue the direction of the offensive action or to bring the screener back toward the basketball. The proper techniques of the pivot and the correct footwork are extremely important, regardless of the types of screens used in a team's offensive repertoire, so that the original screener can smoothly and quickly become a receiver and instant scoring threat. He must be able to quickly face the ball (to be able to receive a quick pass) while also at least partially facing the basket to become an instant scoring threat.

Ball Screen Action

Diagram 6-1 shows the traditional outside ball screen with O1 dribbling off the outside shoulder of O4, who is setting the ball screen. As O4 sets the ball screen, O1 aims for the outside shoulder of O4 (left shoulder, in this instance). After O1 dribble scrapes off O4's ball screen, the action of O4 could be of varying types that will be discussed momentarily.

The more modern inside ball screen with O3 dribbling to the middle or toward the inside off O5's ball screen near the ballside elbow area is shown in Diagram 6-2. After the initial ball screen for O3, the action of the screener (O5) can also vary in many different methods.

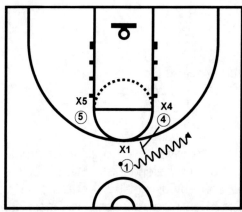

Diagram 6-1

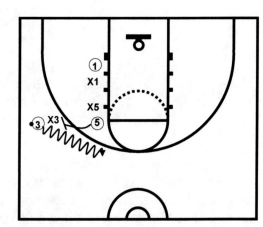

Diagram 6-2

Pick-and-Roll Action

Probably the oldest and most often used offensive action after the ball screen is the traditional pick-and-roll action. Diagram 6-3 shows O4 ball screening the defender of his dribbling teammate (O1). O1 dribble scrapes off the outside (left) shoulder of the ball screener (O4). The scraping of shoulders contact between O1 and O4 signals O4 to open up to the ball (as O1 continues in the original direction) and for O4 to maintain vision of the ball as well as to roll to the basket. The inside (right) foot of the screener (O4) should be the pivot foot (shaded in the diagram), while the outside foot (left) would be the free foot.

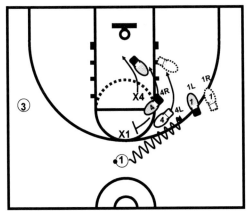

Diagram 6-3

As 01 rubs off the (left) shoulder of 04, 04 should reverse pivot off his inside (right) foot and try to swing the free (left) foot about 90 degrees to seal off his own defender (X4) as he rolls to the basket; while never losing sight of 01 or the basketball. If 01 turns the corner and elects to make the inside pass to his screening teammate (04), 01 could first make a front pivot off his inside (left) foot to face the basket and his teammate rolling to the basket and look to hit 04 on the pick-and-roll.

Reverse and front pivots by both the passer and the pass receiver are essential footwork techniques just for the ball to be passed to the offensive player rolling to the basket. This does not even take into account the offensive post play scoring pivots necessary for the offensive player to use after receiving the ball close to the basket.

Diagram 6-4 illustrates an example of the ball screen set by 04 for his teammate 01. After 01 dribble scrapes off 04's screen, that is the exact time for 04 to reverse pivot and slip the screen and step out to the top of the key. 01 looks to drive and then to pass the ball back to the initial ball screener (04). Since the dribbler should always come off the screener's top shoulder, the top foot of 04 (the left foot) should be the

Diagram 6-4

free foot that swings to open up to be able to continue to see the ball and the passer. Instead of rolling to the basket, 04 swings his free foot approximately 180 degrees. The lower foot (the right foot of 04 in this instance) would be the pivot foot where the reverse pivot originates.

Diagram 6-5 shows 04 first setting a ball screen for 01 and then afterwards going down to set an off-the-ball down screen for 03. 01 again scrapes off the top shoulder of the ball screener, 04. 04 then goes down to headhunt X3 for the down screen. In this case, a front pivot off the lower foot (right foot of 04, in this situation) is the best method for the ball screener. The front pivot with 04's left foot allows him to immediately look for the next defender he is to screen (X3) The reason to use the front pivot in this particular situation is that the front pivot will allow the ball screener (04) to more easily and more quickly locate the defender on (03). In this scenario, 04 is not looking to become a pass receiver/scoring threat, but to screen off the ball to free a different teammate (03) for a potential shot.

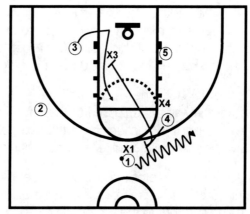

Diagram 6-5

01 should execute proper footwork and pivots so off the ball screen, he can be both a successful shooter as well as a successful passer. For 03 to be successful in getting open as well as being a successful scorer, he also must first get open by executing the proper V-cut fake before cutting off 04's down screen. Upon getting open and receiving the pass from 01, 03 must also use the proper pivot off the inside (left) heel to square up to take an open shot in the lane (off 04's down screen). The dribbler/passer (01), the screener (04), and the pass receiver/shooter (03) must all execute various forms of the proper footwork/pivots for this offensive action to result in a made basket.

Screen-the-Screener Action

Diagram 6-6 shows another one of the more traditional concepts of screens—the screen-the-screener or the pick-the-picker action. In this offensive scenario, 04 initially sets the ball screen on X1, 01's ball defender. After 01 dribbles off the ball screen set by 04, 02 steps up to set an off-the-ball back screen for 04. 04 front pivots off the lower foot (right foot, in this scenario) and steps with his free foot, the left foot. He then should scrape off 02's high shoulder (right shoulder, in this instance) and cuts hard toward the basket while looking over his inside (right) shoulder for the ball to be lobbed to him. The reason to use the front pivot in this particular situation is the front pivot allows the initial ball screener (04) to more easily and more quickly see the passer (01), the basket, and the ball. After 02 sets the screen-the-screener for 04, he should then step out to the top of the key to be a possible shooter or at least a pass receiver for 01.

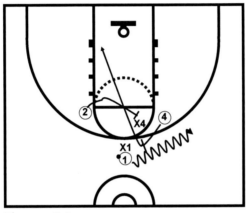

Diagram 6-6

If 04 is not open on his lob route to the basket or the flare cut to the perimeter area, 02 is a secondary outlet receiver who could be a potential perimeter scorer or a conduit that can reverse the ball to the opposite side of the court. After setting the back screen (the screener) for 04, 02 should then have his feet and hands ready to become a potential pass receiver/perimeter shooter. 02 should pivot off his inside (left, in this case) foot if he receives the pass from 01 so he could then make a front pivot to square up to the basket for a possible and potential three-point shot at the top of the key.

At the beginning of this action, 01 should dribble scrape off 04's ball screen, and when dribbling to the offense's right side, 01 should pivot off his inside (left, in this case) foot and square up to the basket as a possible shooter or a passer to any open teammate. Again, the proper pivoting footwork is necessary for all three offensive players involved in this play to be effective scorers or just offensive players.

Off-the-Ball Screeners

The second major category of offensive screens in the today's game of basketball is screens set on defenders who are defending off-the-ball offensive teammates. Many types of off-the-ball screens and many different types of action follow these types of screens. Different types of pivots are required to execute the various kinds of action that follow the initial off-the-ball screens.

Some of the types of screens away from the ball include the following:
- Lane-exchange cross screens (from block to block)
- Perimeter screens away from the ball
- Flare screens
- Back screens
- Spin screens (reverse lane-exchange screen)
- Diagonal down screens
- Flex back screens
- UCLA rub-off screens
- Stagger screens
- Pin screens
- Combination of any of these screens

With the exception of the simple perimeter screens (away from the ball) and the flare screens, every other type of screen mentioned can very easily have subsequent action that may or may not be as important as the initial screen. Every type of action following the initial screen cannot be executed without some form of a pivot (by the initial screener) to initiate that offensive action. Each of these screens and at least one form of complementary action will be discussed and illustrated. A main point of focus that should be stressed to all off-the-ball screeners is for each screener to set the screen so that the backside is pointing directly to the spot where he wants the cutter to cut to get open to receive the ball. The angle of the screen and the position of the actual screener are very important points of emphasis in breaking offensive cutters open to receive the ball to be productive scorers.

Lane-Exchange Cross Screens

Diagram 6-7 illustrates 04's lane-exchange cross screen for 05, followed by the initial screener coming back to the ball (after the defense attempts to switch the screen). Diagram 6-8 illustrates the footwork of the initial screener (04).

04 empties out and goes across the free throw lane and sets this screen on his teammate's defender (X5) with his back to the ball. After 05 sets X5 up with a V-cut, 05 could fake high and scrape off the low shoulder of 04, or 05 could fake low and scrape off the high shoulder of 04. In this scenario, the two post defenders (X4 and X5) will switch men, so that X4 picks up 05 on his cut, and X5 will attempt to defend 04. The shoulder of 04 that 05 scrapes off is the side the switching defender (X4) will

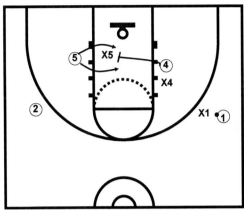

Diagram 6-7

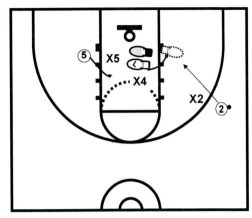

Diagram 6-8

be waiting to then pick up his new offensive responsibility (05). That side is that of the free foot 04 uses to reverse pivot and then seal off his new defender (X5). After pivoting, 04 comes back across the lane to look to receive the ball from 02.

In other words, if the cutter (05) comes off the screen on the high side, the high foot (left, in this case) is the free foot and the lower foot (right, in this instance) is the pivot foot used by 04 to reverse pivot back toward the ball. If the original lane exchange cutter (05) first fakes high and then cuts low (across the lane) off 04's screen, 04's top foot (left) would be the new pivot foot. After making the reverse pivot off the appropriate foot, the original screener (04, in this case) will flash back toward the ball. The original screener-turned-flash-post-player must always make sure that he remains on the notch above the block to be in an efficient offensive threat on the interior. If either offensive player (05 or 04) does receive 02's interior pass, their offensive post moves will require specific footwork and pivoting that has previously been discussed. As a perimeter player and potential passer, 02 also would use the proper pivoting and footwork of a perimeter passer to be successful in delivering the ball to an interior teammate.

Perimeter Back Screens Away From the Ball

Diagram 6-9 illustrates a typical secondary break and also is an excellent example of a (small-on-big) back screen on the perimeter. When the ball is first reversed from 01 on the initial ballside (the left side, in this scenario) to 05 at the top of the key and swung to 02 on the original weakside, the original ballside perimeter player in the corner (03) steps up (with the proper angle) to back screen the defender (X5). Just before the back screen, the original ballside post player (04) should make a series of front pivots and reverse pivots as he cuts and flashes across the lane to chase the basketball and look to receive the ball initially from 03 or subsequently from either 01, 05, or 02.

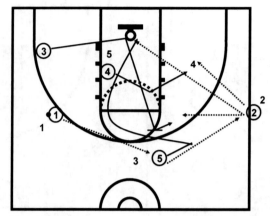

Diagram 6-9

Diagram 6-9 shows the back screen set at the top of the key by 03 for 05. A possible defensive reaction to this back screen is for X3 to switch the back screen and pick up the cutting 05. If X3 switches and picks up 05, 03 can then become a new potential pass receiver and scorer on the perimeter (with a defensive position mismatch—a post defender guarding a perimeter player on the perimeter). This advantage should go to the offense.

Diagram 6-10 shows the perimeter back screen set by 03 and the eventual footwork used to attack the switching defender (X5). After setting the back screen, 03 should front pivot off the foot closest to the ball (the left foot, in this case, with 02 now having the basketball on the right side of the court), step with his right foot inside of X5 to seal off his new defender, and look to receive the ball from 02. This technique makes the screener an immediate pass receiving threat and ultimately a scoring threat to the opposition's defense. After 05 has fully reversed the ball (from 01) to 02 on the opposite side of the court, 05 should prepare for 03's back screen by stepping toward the ball with his ballside foot (right foot, in this scenario) before making a front crossover step off his left foot and scraping off 03's weakside (left, in this case)

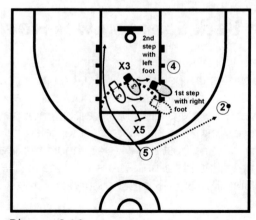

Diagram 6-10

shoulder. He then cuts toward the basket and looks for the lob pass over his ballside (right) shoulder. When 02 receives the ball, the necessary footwork will be required for 02 to be a successful passer to either 05 or to 03 as well as becoming an immediate shooting or driving threat to his own defender.

Spin Screens

Diagram 6-11 demonstrates the end of the secondary break previously described in Diagrams 6-9 and 6-10. After the complete ball reversal (from 03 to 01 to 05 to 02), if 05 does not receive the lob pass, he should step out of the lane to avoid the three-second lane violation and also make sure he is at a lower vertical level than his teammate 04 is on the opposite side of the lane. 02 still can re-reverse the ball to the top of the key to the original back screener (03). After a player sets a screen, the majority of the time that screener is the second offensive player who will be open. In this case, 02 could re-reverse the ball to 03. When that pass is made, the original first trailer (04) again makes the same duck-in cut from the new ballside low-post block to the dotted circle in the middle of the lane. If X4 plays behind him, 03 can easily feed him the ball in the middle of the lane for a high percentage shot. If X4 aggressively defends this second duck-in cut, all of his attention and energy will be on 04 on his duck-in cut. X4 will not see the headhunting lane exchange back screen that 05 will set for 04. With all of the attention that X4 must put on 04 and with the proper angle that 05 must use, this screen is a devastating screen that will free up 04 or 05 or both in the free throw lane. Diagram 6-11 features a spin screen with 05 setting a spin screen on 04's defender (X5).

Diagram 6-12 illustrates the scenario if 04 is successfully fronted by X4 on the duck-in cut on the re-reversal pass from 03 to 02 at the top of the key. 05 would then come across the lane to set what is basically an interior back screen for 04. The original ballside low post player (04) becomes the cutter that uses the reverse pivot off the

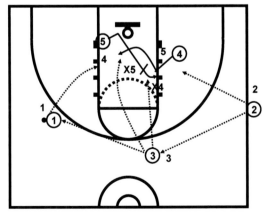

Diagram 6-11

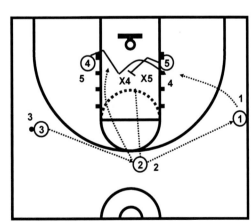

Diagram 6-12

inside foot (left foot in this scenario) to come off the lower side of 05's back screen and cut across the lane to post up on the opposite side.

As this is taking place, the original weakside low post player (05) becomes the back screener that could use a front pivot to get open and to also make himself a second scoring threat. The back screener (05) comes across the lane from the right side of the lane, front pivots off the top foot (left, in this case), and then steps toward 02 and the ball at the top of the key. This screen is called the spin screen, since the cutter (04) always fakes high and cuts low by a reverse pivot and then spinning off the screen.

If 04 spins off 05's screen and cuts off the lower left shoulder of 05, 04 should be able to receive the ball from 01 on the opposite side of the floor. 04 should make sure that he stays above the notch above the block to ensure the best possible angle to attack the basket. Upon receiving the ball from 01, 04 should take a small hop and land with both feet. This technique allows 04 to read where and how his defender is attempting to guard him and also to be able to use either foot as the pivot foot. From there, 04 can continue with his desired post moves that have been previously discussed. During this spin screen action, all three perimeter players (03, 02, and 01) must use proper footwork in handling the basketball as potential shooters or as interior passers. Again, the proper footwork is needed by all five offensive players in order to produce points off this secondary fast break action.

Diagram 6-13 illustrates the footwork by both the spin cutter (04) and the spin screener (05) when the ball is re-reversed from 03 to 02 at the top of the key. On the pass to the top of the key to 02, 04 again makes a strong and aggressive duck-in cut from the ballside block position (on the offense's left side of the lane). 04's steps first with the inside contact foot that is closest to the defender (X4, in this case) (left foot, in this case), then with his outside foot (the right foot) and then again with his contact foot. These three steps position 04 to be higher up into the free throw lane (near the old dotted circle) and further to the middle of the lane. If X4 allows this three-step duck-in cut, 02 should be able to deliver the ball to 04 for a high percentage shot. If X4

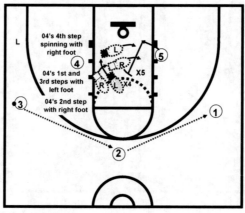

Diagram 6-13

denies this cut, which he should, then 05 can set a blind headhunting back screen on the vulnerable X4 in the middle of the lane. Upon receiving the screen, 04 would then spin low off of 05's low (right) shoulder by reverse pivoting and using his contact foot as the pivot foot and therefore using his free (right) foot to spin 180 degrees off of the screen and then across the lane to post up on the opposite mid-post area.

Diagram 6-13 also illustrates 05 starting at a lower level than 04 before stepping diagonally across the lane to set the back screen on 04's unsuspecting defender. After setting the screen, 05 should be ready to step into his original defender (X5) with his top (left) foot to then post up his defender. If the two post defenders switch this spin screen, 05 should change his footwork and make a front pivot, with his lower (right) foot being the free foot, and rip his new contact arm (right) across his new defender to post him up in the dangerous free throw lane area.

If X5 switches and takes 04 cutting off 05's spin screen, X4 must then also switch to defend his new man (05). 05 should be able to seal off his new defender (X4) with his front crossover pivot (off the top pivot foot). Regardless of whether the interior defenders switch the spin screen or not, 05's final location and positioning will allow him to be in an ideal location in the middle of the free throw lane as well as in excellent position to be able to receive the ball from the top of the key. Having the ball at the top of the key means that there is no true defensive ballside or helpside. Therefore, no definitive helpside defensive support, which X4 most likely would need to adequately stop 04 from receiving the ball and ultimately scoring, is available. Proper footwork after the screen to receive the ball and then the subsequent footwork that 04 would use to then score on his new defender has previously been discussed and should now be used. Because of the simple footwork required by 05 and because of the small amount of spacing available in the free throw lane area, Diagram 6-13 shows only 04's footwork to execute the spin screen cutting action.

Flex Back Screens

Diagram 6-14 illustrates a typical flex back screen along the baseline. This screen is the first of two off-the-ball screens whenever the ball is reversed in the common flex man offense. First, 01 reverses the ball to 05, triggering 04 to set the back screen for 02 cutting along the baseline. Immediately after 04 sets the back screen, 04 goes up and sets his second off-the-ball screen—a back screen for 01. 01 makes a flare cut to the new vacant weakside corner. The more traditional flex back screen action is for 04 to set the back screen for 02 and then for 04 to receive a screen-the-screener down screen by 01. As will be discussed later in the book, this initial offensive action (04's flex back screen followed by 04's flare back screen) can be more productive than the traditional flex action. Therefore, this section will discuss just the footwork for that method of attack.

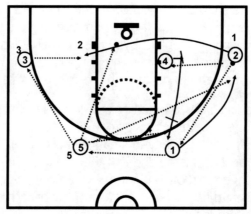

Diagram 6-14

Diagram 6-15 illustrates the footwork of the back screener (04) setting the back screen for 02. Initially, 04 is a post player who is facing the original passer (01). As soon as 01 reverses the ball to 05, 04 must pivot and face 02 with his back pointing toward the middle of the lane to have the proper screening angle to screen X2.

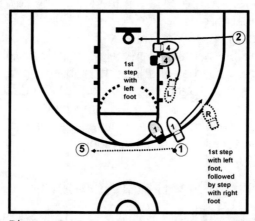

Diagram 6-15

Immediately after the initial flex back screen is set by 04 and is used by the baseline cutter (02), 04 front pivots using the higher foot (the right foot, in this case) as the pivot foot (and, therefore, the lower foot as the foot that swings through on the front pivot). This move is done so that the original back screener (04) can not only more quickly and easily pick up sight of the ball, and the new passer (05) but also X1. 04 should then step up the lane line to flare screen X1 for 01 to then flare cut to the new weakside wing and corner area.

The front pivot by the back screener (04) becomes very important for this particular offensive action. The flex back screen might be defended and, therefore, the next two possible pass receivers/potential scorers would be either 01 off the flare screen and flare cut or 04 to himself after he has slipped his flare screen for 01. This front pivot is the necessary footwork, making this overall flex back screen action more difficult to defend because three possible scorers are now involved, first 02, then 01, and finally 04. The flare screen by 04 and subsequent flare cut by 01 on the perimeter forces X4 and especially X1 to stay more on the perimeter to defend their own men. This approach removes a great deal of congestion in the free throw lane and forces X4 and X1 to make a decision on whether to be stay with their men on the perimeter or be interior support defenders for X2. Whatever decision the opposition makes can be countered by the offense and make that defensive choice a costly mistake for the defense.

Whether the ball is passed to 02 (who has just received the initial back screen) in the lane, or passed to 01 making his flare cut off the second back screen, or passed to 04 who has just set the flex back screen followed by the flare screen, all three offensive players must be prepared to use the necessary pivots to quickly catch and shoot the basketball. The primary pass receiver (02) should realize that he is transitioning himself from a perimeter player momentarily to a post player. He should then be prepared to utilize the necessary footwork in receiving the basketball as well as scoring as an interior post player anywhere in the lane or on the new ballside low-post block. The second two potential scorers (01 and 04) should be preparing themselves to front pivot off their inside foot as perimeter players just as they receive the pass from 05.

After 01 reverses the ball to 05, he should also first V-cut toward the inside (to set his defender up for the upcoming flare back screen by 04) with his inside foot before then planting that inside foot and scraping off 04's flare screen toward the newly declared weakside wing and/or deep corner area (Diagram 6-16). As 01 is making that flare cut, he is already opening up to both the ball and to the basket to get his shoulders squared up, as well as preparing his feet and hands for the pass and following quick shot. This technique allows 01 to more quickly see the basket and see the skip pass coming from 05, so that he can get his perimeter shot off more quickly against the defender (X1) who is pinned in by 04.

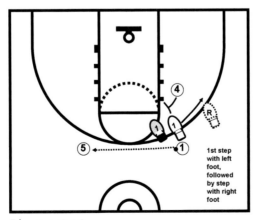

Diagram 6-16

While 02 is the initial primary pass receiver for 05, 04 is also a potential pass receiver/shooter after first setting the initial back screen for 02. On his way up the lane line, 04 should get his feet and hands ready for the possible pass and quick shot. If the ball was not passed to 02 or to 04, 04 could then set the flare screen for 01, allowing 01 to then flare cut and drift to the new weakside corner/wing area. After setting this second screen, 04 could then possibly slip the flare screen for a shot near the elbow area or stepping into the lane for a closer shot, depending on how the opposition's defense handles this offensive action.

Whether 04 chooses to step inside or remain more on the perimeter, 04 becomes the third (after 02 and then 01) viable shooting threat as a result of this offensive action. Upon reading the defenders' reactions, 04 could front pivot off the inside (right) foot and immediately look for a pass from 05. If 04 receives the pass from 05, he should pivot off his inside heel (right, in this case) and make a front pivot to quickly and fluidly square up to the basket and look for his shot or look to pass the ball to another open teammate. Diagram 6-17 illustrates the action as well as the all-important footwork of both 01 and 04.

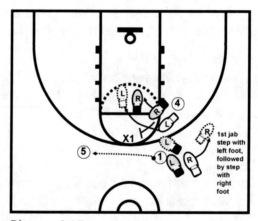

Diagram 6-17

Screen-the-Screener Screens

As previously discussed, a much more typical variation for the flex offense would be for 01 to first reverse the ball to 05 and then go down to set a down screen for 04 (before then drifting out to the weakside deep corner area). This offensive action applies the offensive concept of screening the screener that is difficult to defend.

Because many strong defensive teams teach team defense so that any individual defender is coached to help out their teammates when their specific man screens one of their teammates, the defender on the screener can be easily screened (screen-the-screener concept). This offensive action can then make the screener the primary or at least the secondary pass receiver and scoring threat.

Screen-the-screener action can be very effective, but only when the original screener is taught the necessary footwork to get open and to be able to quickly shoot off the pass after setting the initial screen. Fundamentally sound footwork is necessary for the initial screener to seal his original defender or the switching defender, who is now attempting to guard him. In this action, as shown in Diagram 6-18, 01 reverses the ball to 05, triggering 04 to set the flex back screen for 02. This move is followed immediately by 01 then going down into the free throw lane to set a down screen for 04 to use in this screen-the-screener action.

Diagram 6-19 illustrates 04's footwork after he has set the flex back screen for 02 to use. 04 sets up to receive 01's down screen. After setting the back screen, 04 should make a front pivot off his top (right, in this case) and break up the lane line. As he is doing so, he is getting his feet and hands ready to catch and shoot (off 05's pass). 04 is getting his timing down so that he can pivot off his inside heel (right heel, in this instance) to be able to easily square up to the basket for the medium range shot. 04's footwork is the key to him being able to quickly get the shot off before X4 can recover from helping out on the back screen and then getting down screened himself.

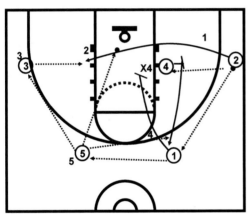

Diagram 6-18

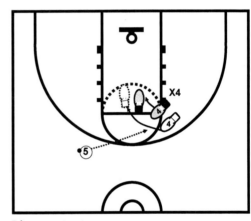

Diagram 6-19

Veer Option From the Flex Screen

Diagram 6-20 shows the action described as the veer action that complements the flex action. This action is very effective in counterattacking a defense that is very concerned with the back screen cutter (03) and forgetting the back screener (05). This option is great for the offense to utilize, particularly when 05 is a good scoring threat inside or when the offense wants to attack and isolate X5 on the interior. This action is much more effective when 03 cuts off 05's seemingly normal flex back screen on the low side, giving 05 the spacing and freedom to duck in to the lane on the high side of his back screen. This cut most likely will influence X5 into actually being lower than 05 so that X5 can hedge, switch or at least help out on the cutting 03. When 05 then ducks in to the free throw lane, this action should have given him position advantage over X5 that must be capitalized on by the offense.

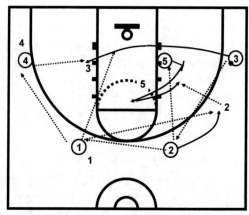

Diagram 6-20

A reverse pivot with the pivot foot being the foot closest to his defender (presumably the left foot, in this instance) into the lane by the initial back screener (05) is devastating to a defense that does not honor or respect the back screener becoming an inside scorer. Triggering this fundamentally sound offensive action, the original ballside guard (02) reverses the ball to the weakside guard (01). As 03 scrapes off 05's back screen, 02 should then make a shallow flare cut to allow for proper spacing. 02's cut decreases the defensive congestion to further isolate X5 or at least to provide himself with an even better passing angle to the veer cutting 05, if 01 cannot deliver the ball to 05 (and must pass the ball back to 02. 02's cut also allows 01 the proper spacing to center up the ball via dribble if 01 chooses, so that he could improve his own passing angle to 05 somewhere near the middle of the free throw lane.

When the original ballside guard (02) reverses the ball to the weakside guard (01), the initial flex back screen (by 05 for 03) is triggered. Regardless of whether the baseline cutter (03) scrapes off 05's back screen on the high (right) or the low (left) shoulder, X5 should probably step over to help on 03's back screen cut to the basket. 05 (with the proper footwork) should have a position advantage on X5 or the switching defender (X3).

05's first steps must not only be into the middle of the free throw lane, but also higher up the lane, which does not just mean up the lane line but also in the middle of the lane. 05's location centers him up and gets him closer to both 01 and 02 as well as giving his passing teammates more open area to lob the ball to 05 if his post defender (X5) wants to three-quarter or fully front 05 in the lane to deny him the ball.

05's ideal location in the lane is crucial to him receiving the pass in high scoring areas and the fundamentally sound proper footwork is what can place him in that location. Because of the proper footwork and pivoting of 05, the position advantage helps him receive the basketball by being able to seal off his defender in high percentage scoring locations. After 03 has cut off the back screen, 05 should step into the center of the lane first with his top foot (right foot, in this scenario). His footwork is similar to very controlled pace of a defensive slide, first with his top foot, then his lower foot, and then followed by his top foot again. By then, he should receive the basketball in the ideal location or be ready to then seal his fronting defender off and then look for the lob pass. After receiving the basketball, 05's offensive post moves (discussed in Chapter 4) consist of other various forms of pivoting and footwork, allowing him to be a high scoring threat on the interior.

If 02 elects to fully reverse the ball to 01, he should make a shallow flare cut and be ready to receive the return pass from 01. 01 should receive the reversal pass from 02 and immediately be in passing, driving, and shooting positions, or in other words, triple-threat position. If that return pass is made by 01 back to 02 after his shallow cut, 02 should immediately be in the triple-threat position to attack X2. To be in the all-important triple-threat position, 02 should pivot off the inside (left) heel so that he can instantly square up to the basket. He should look first to make the inside pass to 04 off 04's veer cut. 02's next option is a quick perimeter shot or the shot fake and drive to the basket.

If the drive to the basket is the offensive choice 02 elects to make, that offensive choice will also require some fundamental footwork. When 02 receives the pass from 01, proper footwork is also necessary for 02 to immediately be in triple-threat position. The top priority for 02 is to catch the reversal pass from 01 and look to pass the ball inside to the veer-cutting 05 or to create with the basketball.

Diagram 6-21 shows the bump option of the flex back screen cut. This action is used to attack defenses that want to switch the flex back screen cut. The bump option effectively allows the offense to retain the original back screener (04, in this scenario) as the post player and the back screen cutter (01) as a perimeter player versus placing this cutter inside.

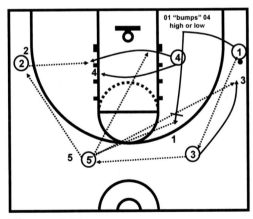

Diagram 6-21

For example, when considering the presumed flex action used where 01 up passes the ball to 03, who then fully reverses the ball to 05, which would the offense prefer: X4 switching to pick up 01 on his flex back screen cut, or 04 posting up X4 inside? Or would the offense prefer for 01 to stay on the perimeter? If 04 stays inside and 01 stays on the perimeter, both players most likely will maximize their offensive skills and talents in the traditional manner—designated perimeter players playing on the offensive perimeter and designated post players playing offensively on the interior.

When 01 is just about to make shoulder-to-shoulder contact with his back screening teammate (04), 01 simply reads how X4 is playing 04. 01 will easily be able to read if X4 is on the low side of 04 or on the high side of 04. If 01 elects for 04 to stay inside, then 01 bumps 04 into the lane by bumping or pushing either shoulder of 04, causing him to reverse pivot by using the foot of the shoulder that was bumped as the free swinging foot (and the opposite foot as the pivot foot). If 01 bumps the top (right, in this case) shoulder of 04, he is telling 04 that his defender is on the low side of him and for 04 to reverse pivot by swinging his top (right, in this case) foot around off his left pivot foot to seal off his defender. After the seal, 04 ducks into the lane and chases the ball. This terminology gives 04 the freedom to cut toward the basketball that is on the perimeter in the hands of either 04 or 02. If 01 bumps the lower shoulder, 04 should reverse pivot off his right pivot foot and look to seal off his defender and swing his low (left) foot around to seal off his man and by being on the low side of his fronting defender (X4). Regardless of what direction 04 goes into the lane, if he receives the ball from any perimeter teammate (05 or 03), he must use the various types of footwork previously discussed to become an effective scoring post player.

The bump action also officially switches 01's cutting assignments with 04's flare screening assignments. 04 chases the ball across the lane in any manner and path he chooses to receive the ball in the lane. 01 either cuts up the lane line to receive 03's down screen (the more traditional bump action) or to set a flare screen for 03 to use (in the preferred manner). Either option places 01 at the new weakside high elbow area as either a potential jump shooter off 05's pass or as a ball reversal man for 05 so that he could then hit 03 on the perimeter or possibly 02 (or 04) on the interior.

01 has the same mindset and the same footwork techniques for either option—that is, to be a potential jump shooter or an interior or perimeter passer. Any perimeter player should have these same techniques when he has the opportunity to possibly receive a pass from a teammate by having his hands ready to receive the ball and being under control enough to pivot off his inside heel (right, in this case) as he catches the 05 pass to become an immediate shooter. 04's footwork as the original back screener is simply to reverse pivot (with the pivot foot being the contact foot) when he is bumped by 01 to seal off his defender and also have his feet and hands ready to catch and score in the paint. After then receiving the inside pass, 04 should then utilize the same proper footwork in being an effective scorer in the paint.

UCLA Rub-Off Screens

Diagram 6-22 shows the action of the UCLA rub-off screen at the high-post elbow area. After 01 passes the ball to 02 at the right wing near the free throw line extended, the ballside high post (04) steps up to set a stationary back screen at the ballside high-post elbow area. After the pass, 01 should V-cut to set his defender up the screen, requiring the proper footwork previously discussed. 01 scrapes off the screen on either the offside or the ballside of the back screen. If 01 does not get the pass from 02, he posts up on the ballside block. If 01 receives the pass, he should utilize the proper offensive post player footwork also previously discussed.

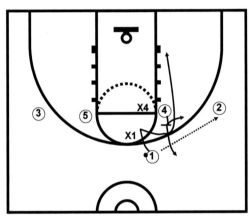

Diagram 6-22

01 must read his defender and take the appropriate path (offside or ballside) to his low-post destination. If X1 does not jump to the ball, 01 could V-cut toward the middle before then rubbing off the outside (left, in this case) shoulder of 04 to look for a quick return pass from 02. If X1 jumps to the ball, 01 could then V-cut toward the ball before then rubbing off the inside (right) shoulder of 04 as he cuts to the basket. A lob pass from 02 to 01 might be in order on this type of cut by 01. 01 V-cuts with either the left or the right foot before then stepping toward the high-post screener with the opposite foot.

Three possible actions 04 could take after setting the back screen rub-off are:
- He could pop out to the top of the key to look for a reversal pass.
- He could front pivot toward 02 and look for the high-post pass.
- He could step out to set an inside ball screen on 02's ball defender.

After setting the screen, 04 could have numerous offensive options, all of which could be very successful as long as the necessary proper footwork is performed and executed.

04 could actually set the UCLA screen with his backside facing 01's defender. The screen could be set (for 01) with the screener (04) either first front or reverse pivoting and facing the basket as soon as 01 makes the pass to 02 on the wing area. One advantage to setting the screen in this manner is the screener (04) is facing the basket and his defender, and also he is able to see the ball and the passer. If his defender (X4) misplays the offensive action, 04 could slip the screen and step toward the basket very effortlessly and quickly for a quick score on 02's pass. Another advantage of the screen being set this way is the screener cannot see the actual defender he is screening (X1), which could help reduce the temptation of 04 moving to set an illegal back screen on X1 to free 01 up off the bat.

Diagram 6-23 shows the footwork used by the screener in the UCLA rub-off screen action. No pivot is made by the screener unless 04 decides to set the UCLA screen with a butt screen—the screen with the screener's butt toward the cutter (01). If that is the case, 04 would have to make a 180-degree front pivot with the inside foot being the actual pivot foot to set the butt screen. This pivot places 04 just inside the (new) ballside elbow area. After 04's screen is set and used by 01, 04 could then make a 90-degree front pivot off the same right foot (that is now on the outside) to face 02 and the ball at the wing and become a true high-post offensive player.

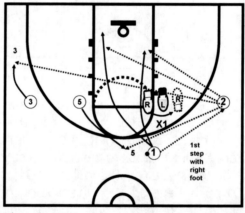

Diagram 6-23

Whether it is 02 making the pass to an open teammate (01, 03, or 05), whether it is 03 or 05 catching the ball on the move, 01 after posting up on the low-post block, or whether it is 04 catching the ball in the new ballside high-post area or after popping out on the perimeter, all pass receivers are potential shooters immediately off the pass from 02. They should properly execute the footwork and techniques of catching the ball and shooting off the pass that have been previously discussed. If 01 receives the inside pass from 02 after posting up, 01 should also use the proper offensive post play footwork already discussed.

Diagram 6-24 shows the action called the UCLA bump at the high-post elbow area. This option is based on an offensive read by 01, who sees how X1 and X4 are attempting to defend the offensive action. If X4 spends more attention and energy on helping his defensive teammate (X1) on his original man and does not honor and respect 04's, then 01 could elect to switch assignments with the original screener (04), which means 01 actually bumps 04 on his originally planned UCLA cut, which dictates that 04 would become the new flash cutter (to the new ballside low-post area). After 01 bumps 04 down to the low post, 01 then replaces himself at the top of the key and remains as a perimeter player. This change of action between 04 and 01 is particularly effective when their two defenders (X4 and X1, respectively) try to anticipate the play and make a defensive switch on the (predicted) UCLA rub-off screen. This option can be used if the coaching staff would rather keep 04 inside and 01 outside because of their individual offensive skills or to outscheme and/or offensively counter the opponent's defensive adjustment. It is a simple and effective move that only involves two offensive players (04 and 01), while the three remaining offensive players all maintain the same locations/positions as well as the exact responsibilities and assignments of the original UCLA rub-off action.

Diagram 6-25 shows the footwork used by the original designated screener (04) in the UCLA bump action. The inside foot (right foot, in this case) should be the pivot foot and a reverse pivot (toward the basket) should be used, with the left foot swinging toward the basket. This step is for 04 to seal off his defender (X4) and create a position advantage over his defender. He then should position himself down in the mid-post area in the new ballside, which allows 04 to always keep his eyes on the ball and the passer (02) as he maintains his position advantage over X4.

After 02 receives the pass from 01, 02 then becomes a potential passer and/or driver/shooter, while it makes 04 a potential low-post player, and leaves 01 as a potential passer and shooter on the perimeter. All three offensive players have to be

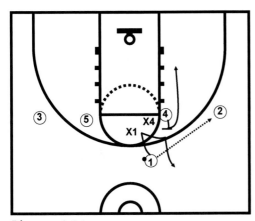

Diagram 6-24

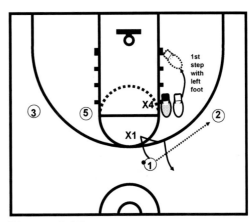

Diagram 6-25

able to execute their own individual proper footwork to make this team offensive action successful. They all have various pivots off a specific pivot foot that must be performed correctly if the action is to produce points for the offensive team.

A major point of emphasis can be to have 01 use the proper footwork to first fake an inside cut off 04's presumed screen before bumping 04 and popping back out to the top of the key. This inside cut could and should have X4 cheat over to shade 04 on the inside so that he could possibly help X1 hedge or switch on 01's presumed cut. Influencing X4 toward the inside will give 04 an even greater opportunity to drop-step and seal off X4 as he slides down to the new ballside mid-post area.

Stagger Screens

Diagram 6-26 shows one of the various forms of stagger screen action set by two off-the-ball players (05 and 01) for a teammate (03). As yet another option, the first screener (05) could slip his screen or break off 01's screen in the form of screen-the-screener offensive philosophy. Slipping the screen is offensive action that is particularly effective when the opposition's defensive players guard the screeners with a hard hedge or sag off to help out on the initial cutter (03).

Diagram 6-27 shows the footwork of the stagger screen action. The stagger screener farthest from the ball (05) should be the first player to screen the original cutter (03). Since he is the first screener, 05 should reverse pivot off the inside pivot foot after 03 scrapes off his outside shoulder. The shoulder of 05 and the moment that the cutter (03) scrapes off determines the pivot foot that 05 uses for his pivot and when he actually makes his pivot back toward the basketball. With 02 having the basketball, 03 is the primary pass receiver for 02 to look for, while the first screener of the stagger screen action (05) is a viable secondary pass receiver/potential scorer for 02 to also look for. Having more than one pass receiver/potential scorer in whatever offensive action is being executed gives the offense more scoring threats.

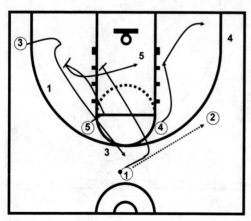

Diagram 6-26

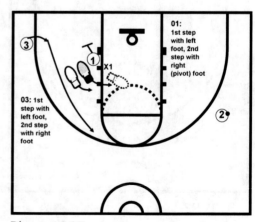

Diagram 6-27

After setting his part of the stagger screen, the reverse pivot by 05 gives him an opportunity to immediately see the new passer and the basketball. The reverse pivot by 05 also allows him a good opportunity to possibly seal off his defender (X5). 05 should set his screen, then reverse pivot off the right foot and actually use 01 as a brush screener to get open somewhere in the free throw lane area. The passer (02) as well as the potential pass receivers/shooters (03 and 05) must execute their individual pivots and proper footwork just to get open, and then after receiving the basketball, they must execute their individual pivots and footwork to be effective scorers.

03 also would have to use the proper pivot and footwork to make the V-cut to set X3 up before receiving the stagger screen. After receiving the pass, 03 would then have to execute the correct footwork as a shooter off the pass.

As stated previously for all pass receivers, 05 would first have to execute the proper pivoting and footwork to get open before having to utilize his offensive post play footwork to be an effective scorer inside. 02 would also have to be ready to use the correct techniques to effectively pivot and pass to his open teammate.

Pin Screens

Diagram 6-28 illustrates one example of a pin screen set by 04 on the ballside low post for 03 cutting across from the opposite side of the court. This type of off-the-ball screen is called the pin screen, with the name being a very accurate description of the screen and its purpose. The screen (by 04) is set on a defender (X3) guarding the offensive player (03), who is cutting toward the ball and away from the basket on the perimeter. The screen actually pins the defender X3 in to allow the cutter an open shot on the perimeter.

After the pin screen is set, the screener (04, in this case) should reverse pivot and become the second potential offensive scoring threat by posting up his defender.

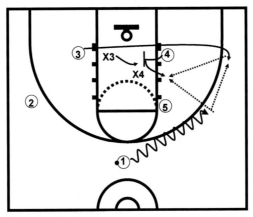

Diagram 6-28

That defender may be his original man (X4), or it may be a new defender (X3) if the defense has chosen to switch on the pin screen. The original cutter (O3) should use the pin screen to receive a pass from O1 and become a potential scorer immediately off the pass or off his dribble drive action. O3 (or O1) could also be a potential passer to the original pin screener (O4) after O4 has sealed off his defender on the block.

Diagram 6-29 shows the footwork of the cutter (O3) who is receiving the pin screen. O3 is cutting toward the ball off the pin screen set by O4, but he also could actually have to move away from the basket on his cut off the screen. As O3 scrapes off the lowest shoulder (right) of O4, O3 should already be getting his feet and hands ready to receive the pass and create immediate action off the pass. As he comes off the pin screen, O3 should have his hands already in position, his shoulders already turning inward toward the passer (O1), and have his steps and footwork down and under control so that he can pivot off his inside heel (right) to do a 180-degree front pivot. This pivot will then allow him to immediately square up to the basket when he actually receives the pass. Upon catching the pass from O1, O3 should square up to the basket in triple-threat position, to either shoot, drive, or pass the basketball to an open teammate (such as O4).

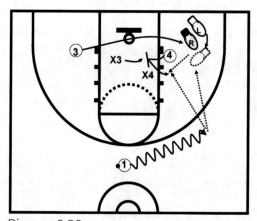

Diagram 6-29

The second potential scorer in this particular pin screen action is for the original pin screener (O4). Initially, O4 pin screened teammate O3's defender (X3), and this screen is a very difficult type of screen for X3 to get around, particularly if O3 has used good fakes and V-cuts to set X3 up. Many defensive teams will have taught defenders to help out on this type of screen, which means that X4 might have to hedge out, switch, or fake a switch and attempt to help out his defensive teammate who is in trouble (X3). Any defensive movement by X4 to help his teammate (X3) defend the cutter can easily put X4 in a poor location to adequately defend his own man. If X4 helps on the low (baseline) side of the pin screen, he could easily get caught on the low side of O4 when O4 slips the pin screen to then post his own defender up in a very opportune scoring location: the mid-post block area. If X4 helps out on the high side of 04's screen, X4 should get stuck on the high side of 04, which can again be a very dangerous predicament for X4. If X4 simply switches the pin screen action with X3, 04 should even more easily be able to begin a position advantage on his new defender (X3). Whoever is stuck with the chore of defending 04, proper pivoting and footwork will allow 04 to maintain that position advantage to receive the ball. As stated countless times, proper footwork and pivoting techniques will provide 04 with a great deal of scoring opportunities after receiving the inside pass from an offensive teammate.

01 or 03 both become perimeter players that are obvious potential passers. Both of these players also need to execute the pivoting footwork of passers discussed earlier to be able to successfully deliver the ball to an interior offensive teammate, particularly 04 in this scenario.

After pin screening for his teammate, 04 should immediately reverse pivot off his contact foot, which is the foot closest to his defender (X4) by swinging his opposite free foot around to seal his defender off and to then post up with the new position advantage he has gained on his man (Diagram 6-30). The reverse pivot allows the pin screener immediate vision of the ball and passer as well as the position advantage over the specific defender that is attempting to guard him. If X4 is playing on the high side of the pin screen, the technique of reverse pivoting and using the top foot (in this case, it is the left foot) as the pivot foot (and making the lower foot or the right foot the free foot) allows 04 to have more room in the low post. 04 now has more room to operate and more room to better receive the pass as well as much better drop-stepping and shooting angles to the basket. 01 could pass the ball directly to 03 (the pin screen cutter) for the perimeter shot, or directly to 04 (the actual pin screener) posting up after he has set the pin screen.

03 could catch the pass from 01 and look to shoot immediately off the catch. But if a defender rushes out to take away 03's perimeter shot, 03 could then shot fake and make the inside pass to 04 posting up inside on the low-post block.

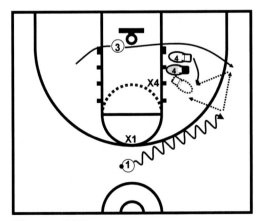

Diagram 6-30

Any of these offensive scenarios can be very proficient in scoring points for the offensive team. As mentioned time and again in this book, the proper footwork and pivoting techniques and skills would be required for O1 (after killing his dribble and looking to make the assist to an open teammate), for the pin screen cutter (O3) to first get open and then to be able to quickly shoot off the pass, for O3 to instead become a driver or inside passer (to O4), or for the pin screener (O4) to either be the primary or at least the secondary pass receiving and scoring threat. Footwork is of utmost importance in all of these offensive actions.

Teaching Methods

The importance of the techniques of proper footwork and of pivoting is mentioned over and over again for one basic reason: footwork and pivoting skills are absolutely essential in having offensive success both on the perimeter area as well as in the post area. These skills are required for players wanting to pass the ball, take shots, or attack the basket. Talking about it is one thing, and coaches (and players) committing to making sure every player has these necessary skills is another. These skills must be first taught by coaching staffs at all levels and then practiced repeatedly, in many different types of drills and situations. Players must not only be observed by coaching staffs with a keen eye to detail, but also critiqued in a serious but positive manner. The techniques must be drilled constantly with many repetitions and in different forms of drills. The eventual final phase of drills must be performed in as close to game conditions as possible. That means the drills must include competition (either against other individuals or other groups) and the drills must require all players to always execute the drills at game speeds. Every drill must integrate maximum game-realistic conditions for both players and coaches to get their money's worth.

One of the best methods to teach basketball skills and techniques is the whole-part-whole teaching method. This effective teaching method can be described in the following manner. A particular basketball skill or technique should be initially introduced to the team and then each player's responsibilities are demonstrated to every player on the squad. Then, coaches should have every player walk through the technique under the scrutiny of the coaching staff. Players learn best by doing. Players can ask questions, and coaches can then answer them before moving on to the next phase.

After the walk-through of the entire concept, those same movements of the players are sped up to a quicker pace. Then, more game-realistic breakdown drills are incorporated to work on those very specific techniques. When proficiency is shown by players, the same drills should be executed at an even quicker pace until game speed is reached. Afterwards, the individual players can be brought back together to run through the skills in a team setting. The degree of difficulty that the practice defensive team places on the practicing offensive team should increase as the offensive team improves and their confidence level increases.

For instance, the actual breakdown drills could first include a dribbler/passer with the ball, an offensive screener, an offensive cutter or the offensive post player, and a dummy defender on the ball handler and the pass receiver. Coaches should stress to the dummy defender not to exert a large amount of defensive energy at the beginning of the series of breakdown drills. As the offensive players improve and progress in their execution of that particular offensive skill, the defensive players should step up their efforts to provide for a more challenging scenario (and more game realism). In this scenario, a later breakdown drill would be to add a dummy defender on the actual screener (to make the scenario more realistic and more challenging to every offensive player involved in the drill).

Some of these breakdown drills could end up having a minimum of at least three offensive players and two defensive players. Coaches should be reminded to rotate all players into the drill and to use both the offensive as well as the defensive side of the ball when utilizing the breakdown drills for the various screening methods. Breakdown drills are used for a short periods of time to maximize time efficiency and mental alertness as well as productivity. Coaching staffs can always come back and drill again later in practice to further improve players' skill levels.

One example of a mass footwork drill is illustrated in Diagram 6-31. This drill incorporates three four-man groups (an entire 12-player team) with defenders on the perimeter ball handlers. Coaches can place limitations on how many dribbles the offense practice player can use and can limit what the offensive post player can do wants he receives the pass.

After a period of 55 seconds, all four players in a group have a five-second period to quickly and immediately rotate to the next position in that drill. In a matter of just four minutes, all four spots can be covered, meaning each player can work on the four different phases of the drill.

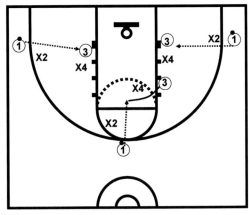

Diagram 6-31

Later in the same practice, this mass drill can be repeated two or more times with each four-man group having to start in a different location. In 12 minutes of practice, each player will be able to work on offensive footwork both as a perimeter passer/ feeder and as an offensive post player receives the pass and attacks the basket with various offensive post moves. The skills and techniques will become second nature, and all offensive players will have a great chance of becoming very proficient in both perimeter and interior offensive skills—making each player a well-rounded offensive basketball player.

Summary

As vital of a concept as screening is to overall offensive schemes, the art of pivoting is the most significant part of the screening skill. As stated time and again, proper footwork and proper techniques, in general, allow players to have a much greater opportunity of succeeding as individual basketball players. Using the whole-part-whole teaching method, all players will become as proficient in the various offensive skills and techniques as they possibly can. And remember: "Your team is only as good as its weakest link."

Important Pivots
of the Defender

"Offense wins games, but defense wins championships."
—Anonymous

Another old basketball adage that many coaches adhere to is: "Offenses win games, but defense wins championships." Without a doubt, defense is extremely important in the overall success of a basketball team. To perform well as a team defensively, every individual player on the defensive team must be able to defend well as well as perform the many other defensive techniques that are necessary for overall defensive success.

On-the-Ball Defensive Pivots

A good team defense must have several very good on-the-ball defenders. For a defensive player to be a good ball defender, that defender must be able to constantly pressure the opponent's dribbler/passer. When the opposition's ball handler changes direction, the on-the-ball defender must be able to immediately change direction and instantly maintain that high degree of defensive pressure on the dribbler.

Most offensive ball handlers have been taught to attack the lead foot of the ball defender. Diagram 7-1 illustrates the lead or the front foot of the ball defender to be the right foot. If the dribbler attacks the lead foot, the dribbler is attacking the defender's right foot or the right side of the defender.

Diagram 7-1 illustrates the offensive player (who has his right foot as his pivot foot and his left foot as his free foot) attacking the defender's lead (right) foot with what offenses sometimes call a blast move—a straight-ahead drive with the offensive player's free foot (left) stepping straight forward toward the basket and that defender. Notice that even though this discussion concerns the footwork of the ball defender, it cannot be helped to also mention the footwork of the opposition's offensive ball handler. *You cannot get away from the footwork techniques and concepts, both defensively as well as offensively.*

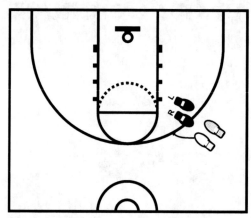

Diagram 7-1

Diagram 7-2 demonstrates how the offensive ball handler could have also attacked the ball defender's same lead foot with a front crossover move (if the offensive player's right foot were the free foot.)

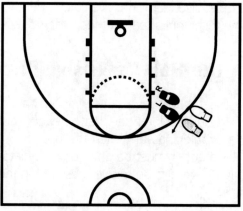

Diagram 7-2

Diagrams 7-3 and 7-4 show that the first step the ball defender should make is to drop-step toward the direction of the dribbler's initial attacking move. This defensive reactionary move is with the ball defender's lead foot, which is the defender's right foot, making a 90- to 135-degree reverse pivot. This pivot is done by swinging the lead (right) foot back and using the trail foot (left foot, in this example) as the pivot foot. The initial footwork by the defender is supplemented by the defender swinging the lead arm (right arm) back to initiate the momentum of the drop-step of the lead foot.

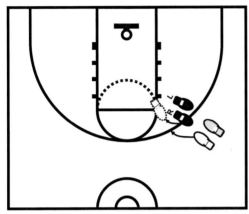

Diagram 7-3

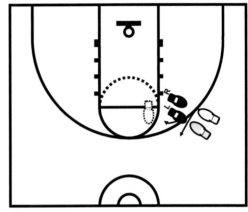

Diagram 7-4

After the lead foot drop-steps, the pivot (left) foot should be used to push very hard in the new direction the defender wants to go. The lead foot drop-steps and steps out as the new trail foot, while the left foot (in this instance) is actually the (reverse) pivot foot and the new push-off foot. This technique is what is called the drop and swing step and the push-push method. If this method is executed precisely with every minute technique performed properly, the ball defender will increase his quickness in his defensive movements and reactions to the opposition's dribble penetration toward the basket.

Most likely, the ball handler will change direction of his dribble as soon as the defender executes his proper footwork and defensive techniques to cut off the dribbler. The phrase that coaching staffs should constantly tell the ball defenders is: "Physically you are here, while mentally you are there." That tells the ball defender to then mentally anticipate the dribbler to change directions once the defender has cut off the dribbler's initial path. This helps mentally prepare the defender to make another reverse pivot, drop and swing step, and use the push-push technique to continue defending and pressuring the dribbler.

Breakdown Drills

Three very valuable and productive breakdown drills that coaching staffs should use to improve the man-to-man (as well as zone and zone press) defensive skills and techniques are called:

- Push-push drill
- Push-and-talk drill
- Pride drill

In addition to several other defensive techniques and fundamentals, all three of these drills stress and emphasize basic defensive fundamental footwork involving the reverse pivot technique and the subsequent pushing off of the next lead foot that is required to play strong defense successfully.

The push-push drill (Diagram 7-5) is a mass defensive drill stressing the four basic movements of individual defenders. The basic foot movements of a ball defender consist of: the advance (towards the offense) step, the drop-and-swing step, the push-off step, and the slide-step.

In the advance step, the defender pushes off his back foot and strides forward a step toward the ball handler. This defensive footwork occurs either when the opponent's ball

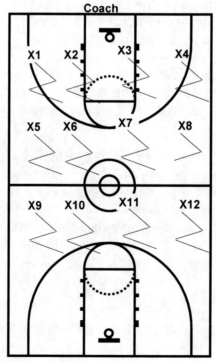

Diagram 7-5

handler retreats from his stepping forward in his own offensive rocker step or when the ball defender elects to put more pressure on the opponent's offensive ball handler.

In the drop-and-swing step, the defender pushes off his initial lead foot to either retreat or to react to the opponent's attack. This defensive drop-step is to prevent the attacker from gaining a greater advantage from his offensive forward thrust off his rocker step or from gaining a further advantage after the attacker has started his dribble drive.

The push-off step follows the defensive drop-step, and its name accurately describes its action. The new lead foot after the reverse pivot and drop-step is the foot that generates the power for the defender to push off in the direction that he must steer toward to cut off of the opposing dribbler's direction. The power of the push-off step is what provides the quickness of the ball defender in his reaction to the offensive ball handler.

In the slide-step, the defender has already drop-stepped with his reverse pivot and then pushed off of his new trail foot (the original lead foot) and slides in the direction of the dribbler's new path toward the basket. As always, the defender wants to keep his body between the dribbler and the basket.

The push-push group defensive drill can and should be utilized to educate and teach all defenders how to properly use the footwork techniques and also how to repetition those techniques in a time-efficient and somewhat game-realistic manner. Two phases are involved in this particular defensive breakdown drill. The first phase is when the coach stands in front of the group of defenders. The coach simulates being the opponent that has a basketball. That coach begins by simply making fakes off his rocker step. The defenders in the mass drill use the appropriate step to defend the movement of the rocker step. That coach must be mindful to use both his left and his right foot as the foot to use for his rocker step.

The second phase is when the coach actually begins his dribble. The defenders in the mass drill must quickly react and move to stay in front of the imaginary dribbler that the drill coach is attempting to simulate. Each defensive practice player works on the proper techniques, including using the appropriate footwork and pivoting. Quickness and effort are also important points of emphasis that the coaching staff constantly observes and evaluates.

The push-and-talk drill (Diagram 7-6) depicts a defender having to sometimes use the advance step, followed by the drop-and-swing step, then the push-off step with the subsequent slide. These steps are to be executed while running through a maze of obstacles and six distinct changes of directions. The diagram shows X1 running the advance step to the mid-court near point A. X1 then uses the drop-and-swing step, the push-off step and finally the slide-step to end up at the free throw line. X1 slide-steps and pushes as quickly and as hard as he can until he reaches point D. Then, X1 changes direction by using another drop-and-swing step (with the left foot being the pivot foot), followed by a push-off step (with the left foot) and several more slide-steps across the court to point E. After reaching point E, he then makes another drop-and-swing step (this time with the right foot being the pivot foot), a push-off step (with the right foot) and slide-step back to the center of the free throw lane before then pushing off back to the original baseline.

Following is the maze part and the more game-realistic part of the drill. X2 begins his slide when X1 reaches the free throw line for the second time. X3 begins his slides when X2 reaches the free throw line his second time. X4 and X5 repeat the process. So it is easy to see that five defenders are doing slide-steps at the same time. This forces all defenders to still execute the proper footwork and techniques, while keeping their head up and their eyes open, and it also forces each defender to communicate and to avoid collisions with teammates.

Diagram 7-7 is the zigzag pride drill. In this drill, the defenders must keep the offensive ball handlers contained and under control in a more difficult setting: the full court. X1 defends 01. X2 defends 02. X3 defends 03, and so forth. All three pair of practice players must stay within the dribbling alleys and the confines shown. 01 tries to beat X1 off the dribble, as do the other two pairs of practice players. X1 must turn 01 at least three times up the court. X1 does this by using the appropriate defensive footwork and techniques previously discussed. X1 must get in front of 01 and draw

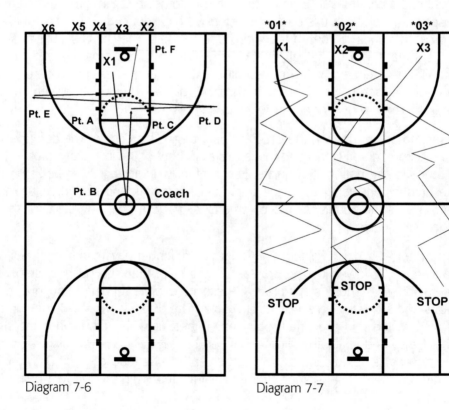

Diagram 7-6   Diagram 7-7

the charge if O1 does not change directions. X1 cannot get lazy and reach for the basketball, but instead, he must move his feet and stay balanced. X1 must never allow O1 to beat him on the dribble and squeeze by him on one of the edges of his dribble alley. Coaches can make this drill even more difficult for the defender by requiring the defender to lock his hands behind his back to prevent the bad habit of reaching for the ball and therefore becoming off balance, lazy, and not willing to move the feet and committing lazy reaching fouls. This modification would require X1 to use his footwork to become quicker and more of a defensive hustler.

To prevent boredom of players and, more importantly, to provide for a more game-realistic defensive drill, the start points and finish points of the pride drill can and should constantly be changed. Various offensive scenarios for the ball handler to start his dribbling could include any of the following:

- Receiving a skip pass that the ball defender first must close out on the new ball handler
- Receiving a hypothetical screen off the ball and then being allowed to receive the pass
- Receiving a ball screen that then initiates his dribble
- Facing a defender who starts as an off-the-ball defender that executes a defensive help-and-recover situation
- Any other situations that a creative coach can dream up

Various offensive scenarios that could and should be utilized for the ball defender to work on and improve specific defensive techniques (at the conclusion of the dribble and the end of the dribble alley) could include any of the following:

- Guarding an offensive ball handler with a killed dribbler
- Taking a defensive charge
- Diving for a loose ball
- Boxing out an offensive ball handler who takes a jump shot off the dribble
- Jumping to the ball after a killed dribble
- Denying give-and-go cuts to the basket
- Other scenarios that an imaginative coach could think of

Footwork Used in Traps

If a coach has a philosophy of utilizing various forms of double-team traps anywhere on the court, whether it is in the full-court press phase or the half-court trap defensive phase, the technique of pivoting is an important part of the trapping process. Every defender involved in the initial trap should release from the trap and react to the location of the escape pass. Some trappers should immediately shift to specific locations off the ball, while other trappers follow the pass to trap again.

All trappers should use the proper technique of pivoting after the escape pass is made. The simplest way to explain the technique is for the coaching staff to tell each trapper to reverse pivot off the outside foot, therefore swinging the inside foot away from the passer toward the location of the escape pass. Each trapper should have it stressed to him to pivot quickly after the escape pass and *not* to look at the flight of the ball before reacting to the landing spot, but to anticipate where the escape pass will land and immediately pursue the flight of the ball by trying to beat the pass to its location. Without proper footwork, this difficult defensive goal would be impossible to achieve or even come close to achieving.

Diagram 7-8 shows two defensive trappers (X1 and X2) trapping the opponent's offensive guard (O1). When O1 escape passes to O2 in the deep corner, X4 closes out to get ready to build a new trap. X2 releases out of the initial trap to re-trap with X4. X2 tries to beat the ball to its potential new location. X1 releases out of the trap and rotates to a new position off the ball to become a different type of team defender in the defensive trap package.

Diagram 7-9 shows the footwork of the two trappers (X1 and X2). X1 reverse pivots (away from the actual opposition's ball handler) off of the right (outside) foot, while X2 also reverse pivots (away from the same ball handler) off the left (outside) foot to go re-trap the ball with X4 in the deep corner.

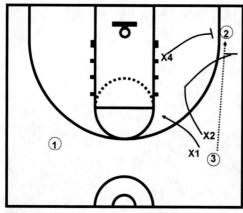

Diagram 7-8

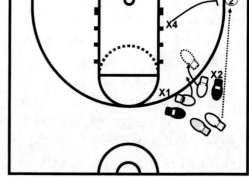

Diagram 7-9

Defensive Rebounding Footwork

Still another time that the use of pivots is a needed ingredient in a team's defensive system is the defensive rebounding part of the game. This footwork was detailed in Chapter 5. However, for completeness sake, it is mentioned again. This part of a team's defense should be utilized every time the opponents shoot and miss their shot, regardless of whether the team is in a man-to-man defense or in any type of zone or trapping style of defense.

Diagram 7-10 shows an example of several off-the-ball defenders making successful defensive box-outs before the defensive rebound is secured. Only the on-the-ball defender (X1), who is guarding the shooter (01), should make the front pivot before going after the defensive rebound. The four off-the-ball defenders are the defenders who should all make the reverse pivots to properly execute the all-important defensive box-outs that are necessary to secure the defensive rebound. Specifically, X2 and X3 are the two defenders who are one pass away; with X4 being a ballside post defender, and X5 being the only helpside defender sagging off in the lane.

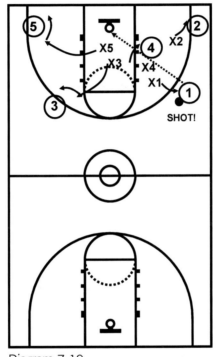

Diagram 7-10

Grabbing the defensive rebound concludes the end of the opposition's possession, and it begins the possession of the ball for that original defensive rebounding team. This move halts the scoring chances of the opposition and begins the scoring opportunities of the initial defensive team.

After the defense has successfully boxed out the offensive opponents and has grabbed the defensive rebound, that defensive rebounder must then make an outlet pass to a teammate to begin the fast break. If the fast break style is not utilized by that team, the outlet pass must still be used to get the ball into a guard's hands to bring the ball down the court slowly and carefully. To make the outlet pass successfully, the defensive rebounder must make a front pivot, The defensive rebounder's front pivot actually is initially turning away from the opposition's pressure on the ball since the defensive rebounder at the beginning, has his back turned toward the opponent. This front pivot must be made for the rebounder to sight the outlet pass receiver and the location of the location of pass receiver defenders before the outlet pass can actually be made.

Diagram 7-11 shows a defensive rebounder gaining possession of the rebound on the opponent's right side of the court. The defensive rebounder (X2) has successfully boxed out his man (as have the other four defenders) and obtained the rebound. X2 should chin the ball (as offensive post players are taught to do when catching the inside pass) and to front pivot away from the opposition's ball pressure. This front pivot should be executed off the outside foot (in this case, the right foot) and the inside foot (left) should then turn away from potential opposing defenders (02 and 05). This front pivot is also made to face the outlet receiver (X1) before making the pass to him.

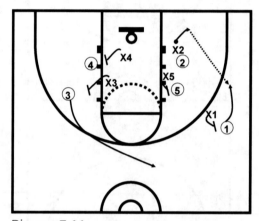

Diagram 7-11

It must be kept in mind that the pass receiver catching X2's outlet pass (X1) must meet the pass before catching the ball. Upon receiving the outlet pass from X2, X1 should also make a front pivot toward the sideline (away from potential defenders located in the middle). This move should be done by front pivoting (away from the opposition's ball pressure) off the outside foot (right foot, in this case) and swinging the inside (left) foot toward the sideline, while also chinning the ball.

Diagram 7-12 shows a defensive rebounder (X2), who has made the defensive box-out and grabbed the defensive rebound. The outlet pass is made to the guard (X1), who also front pivots off the outside pivot foot (left) and swings the inside free foot (right) toward the outside (away from crowd of defenders located in the center of the court). X1 can then see his basket at the other end of the court. He can also quickly and easily spot any teammates ahead of him (X3, in this example).

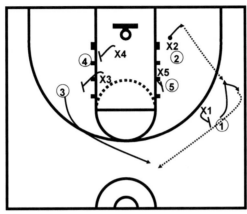

Diagram 7-12

Summary

As important of a concept as defending the ball is to the overall defensive schemes and as important as defensive box-outs and actual outlet passes from the defensive rebound are, the art of pivoting is most important to all three parts of the team defense.

Conclusion: The Overall Importance of the Pivot

If a basketball player or coach truly examined the many different techniques, concepts, and skills that are required for a player and for the team to be successful, he should realize the extreme overall value and importance of the pivot and footwork in basketball.

Offensive players, such as post players with the ball, must not only know the various types of footwork, but be able to execute those skills. Offensive post players must also how, when, and where to use the various kinds of footwork to actually get open so they can become scorers (or eventually passers) for their offensive team.

To counter offensive players with and without the ball, defensive post players must also acquire the knowledge and skills of being able to execute their desired footwork.

Offensive and defensive perimeter players also have various types of footwork mandatory for their overall success. This footwork for offensive perimeters comes from being cutters, screeners, passers, dribblers, and shooters, while defensive perimeter players must have the necessary footwork to counter their offensive opponents' executions of the various offensive concepts and techniques.

Rebounding, both on the offensive end as well as the defensive end of the court, mandates specific types of pivots and footwork for players on both sides of the ball.

These countless types of footwork, along with the many forms of pivoting, are requirements for individual players to be successful in the many different phases of the game. When all players are proficient in each of these phases of the game, their defensive and offensive performances will be successful. When a team is successful in both their offensive and defensive executions, their team will be successful and win many games.

Coaches must first be students of the game and learn the different types of footwork and pivots—their strengths, weaknesses, and when, where, and why to use them. Coaching staffs must then sell the value and importance of footwork to every team member. Coaches must be able to explain, teach, practice, drill, and correct every player in every one of the phases of the game. A coach cannot teach what he does not know. Players must accept the philosophies and the teachings of their coaching staff to continually improve and become successful in their executions of the many types of techniques, both offensively as well as defensively.

About the Author

John Kimble began his basketball coaching career as an assistant basketball coach at Lexington (IL) High School. He was the head freshman coach, the head freshman-sophomore coach, and the assistant varsity basketball coach. During that season, each squad lost only two games and all three squads amassed an overall 61-6 record, with the varsity losing in overtime in the state tournament's Elite Eight round.

The following year, Kimble took the head basketball coaching position at Deland-Weldon (IL) High School, where the varsity accumulated a five-year record of 91-43 that included two regional championships, two regional runners-up, and one sectional tournament runner-up. From there, he moved to Dunlap (IL) High School. His five-year record at Dunlap amounted to an overall 90-45 record that included two regional runners-up, one regional championship, one sectional and one super-sectional championship, and a final second place finish in the Illinois Class A State Tournament.

Kimble then moved to Florida, where he became an assistant basketball coach at Central Florida Community College in Ocala, Florida. The next year, he became the offensive coordinator in charge of the team's overall offense. For the next two years, he retained that offensive coordinator responsibility while also becoming the associate head basketball coach, with a two-year record of 44-22. The four-year overall record while at CFCC was 73-58.

Kimble then became the head basketball coach at Crestview (FL) High School for the following 10 years. Excluding the initial year, the overall record averaged almost 18 wins each year for the next nine years.

Kimble has worked close to 100 weeks of basketball camps and has spoken at several coaching clinics and camps. He also has had over 70 articles published in the following publications: *The Basketball Bulletin of the National Association of Basketball Coaches, The Scholastic Coach and Athletic Journal, Coach and AD, Winning Hoops,* and *Basketball Sense,* as well as contributing articles submitted and all diagrams drawn for NABC's *Coaching Basketball* in two separate editions.

Kimble has authored four other books published by Coaches Choice: *The Basketball Coaches' Complete Guide to Zone Offenses, The Basketball Coaches' Complete Guide to the Multiple Match-Up Zone Defense, Coaching Basketball's Multiple 2-1-2 Full-Court Zone Press,* and *Coaching Basketball's "Speed Game" With Primary and Secondary Fast Breaks.* He has also made four different series of DVDs on various topics of the game.

After 25 years of coaching basketball and several years of coaching baseball and football, Kimble is currently teaching math classes at Crestview (FL) High School, still studying the game, and still writing various basketball articles and books.